MARCO

CHANNEL ISLANDS

JERSEY GUERNSEY
HERM SARK ALDERNEY

www.marco-polo.com

THE TOURING APP

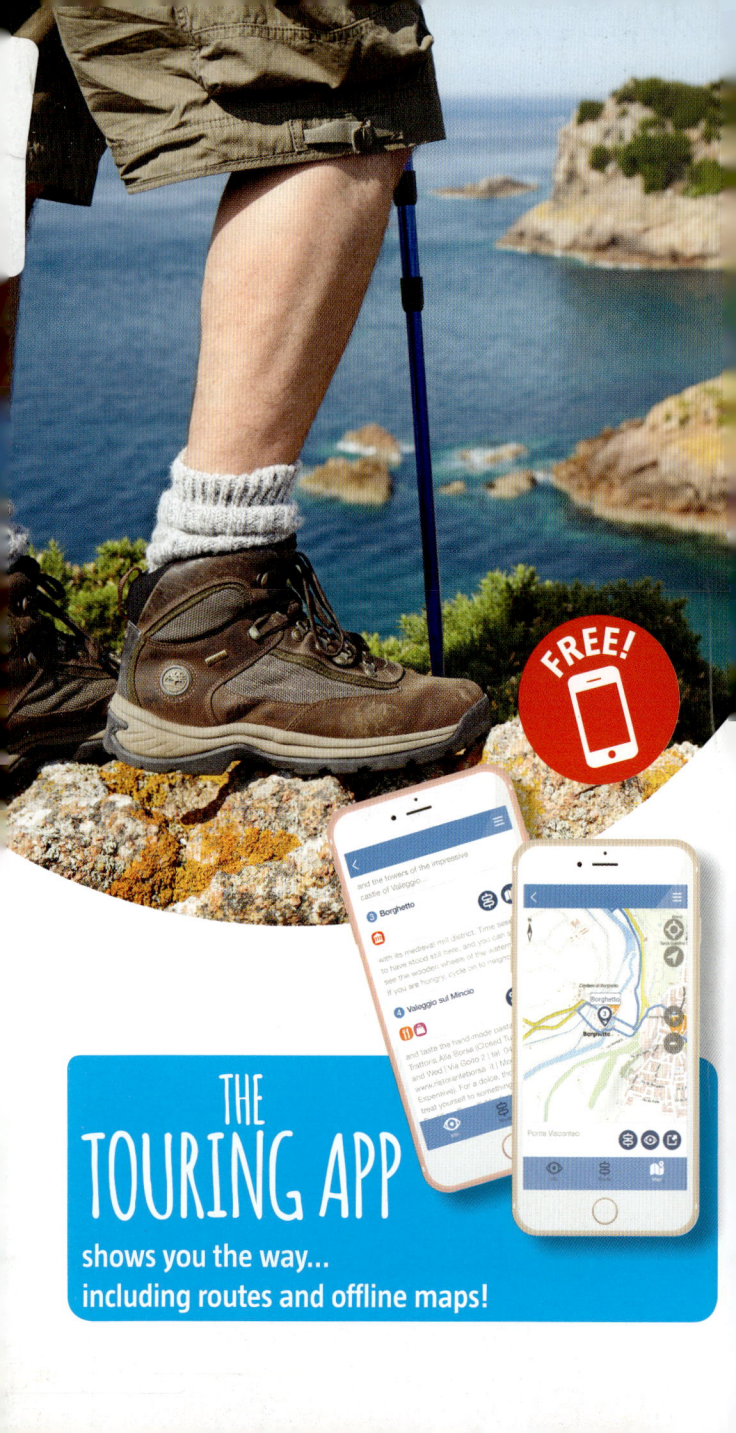

shows you the way...
including routes and offline maps!

FREE!

GET MORE OUT OF YOUR MARCO POLO GUIDE

IT'S AS SIMPLE AS THIS

1 go.marco-polo.com/cis

2 download and discover

GO!

WORKS OFFLINE!

6 **INSIDER TIPS**
Our top 15 Insider Tips

8 **BEST OF …**
- Great places for free
- Only on the Channel Islands
- And if it rains?
- Relax and chill out

12 **INTRODUCTION**
Discover the Channel Islands!

18 **WHAT'S HOT**
There are lots of new things to discover on the Channel Islands

20 **IN A NUTSHELL**
Background information

26 **FOOD & DRINK**
Top culinary tips

30 **SHOPPING**
For a fun-filled shopping spree

32 **JERSEY**
33 The West
38 The North
43 The East
46 The South
51 St Helier

58 **GUERNSEY**
60 The South
65 The West
69 The North
72 St Peter Port

80 **ALDERNEY**

SYMBOLS

INSIDER TIP Insider Tip
★ Highlight
●●●● Best of …
🌿 Scenic view
✪ Responsible travel: fair trade principles and the environment respected
(*) Telephone numbers that are not toll-free

PRICE CATEGORIES HOTELS

Expensive over £160
Moderate £115–£160
Budget under £115

Prices are based on a double room with breakfast during the high season.

PRICE CATEGORIES RESTAURANTS

Expensive over £22
Moderate £12–£22
Budget under £12

Prices are based on an average main course.

4

CONTENTS

88 HERM & SARK
 88 Herm
 91 Sark

98 DISCOVERY TOURS
 98 The Channel Islands at a glance
 103 Jersey by bicycle
 105 On foot along Jersey's north coast
 108 Coastal walk near St Peter Port

110 SPORTS & ACTIVITIES
Activities for all seasons

114 TRAVEL WITH KIDS
Best things to do with kids

116 FESTIVALS & EVENTS

118 LINKS, BLOGS, APPS & MORE
Plan ahead and use on the go

120 TRAVEL TIPS
From A to Z

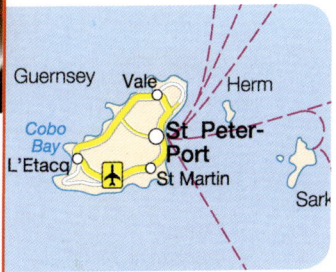

124 ROAD ATLAS

134 INDEX & CREDITS

136 DOS AND DON'TS

DID YOU KNOW?
Timeline → p. 14
For bookworms and film buffs → p. 23
Local specialities → p. 28
Living in forts and towers → p. 52
Daily coastal picnic → p. 57
Beautiful bills → p. 66
Public holidays → p. 117
Currency converter → p. 121
Weather → p. 122
Budgeting → p. 123

MAPS IN THE GUIDEBOOK
(126 A1) Page numbers and coordinates refer to the road atlas
(U A1) Coordinates for the maps of St Helier and St Peter Port can be found in the back cover

Coordinates are also given for places that are not marked on the road atlas

(*A–B 2–3*) Refers to the removable pull-out map
(*a–b 2–3*) Refers to additional inset maps on the back of the pull-out map

INSIDE FRONT COVER:
The best Highlights

INSIDE BACK COVER:
Maps of St Helier and St Peter Port

5

The best MARCO POLO Insider Tips

Our top 15 Insider Tips

INSIDER TIP Magical caves at low tide

The caves on Jersey's north coast are only accessible to kayakers – all except for the *rock grotto at Plémont Beach*. When it's raining, the entrance is marked by a waterfall → **p. 42**

INSIDER TIP A snack bar with a difference

You have to try the local oysters at least once. Sean *Faulkner* serves this classy shellfish in unpretentious style from a rustic Second World War bunker with a sea view. It's situated on Jersey's west coast → **p. 36**

INSIDER TIP A fruity tipple

At the Hamptonne Country Life Museum (photo top), don't forget to fill a bottle of *home-brewed cider*: dry and hearty → **p. 47**

INSIDER TIP Lodgings for an island VIP

In the old fortress *La Crête Fort* above Bonne Nuit Bay on Jersey's north coast, you can stay in the "boutique" setting → **p. 43**

INSIDER TIP VW camper van nostalgia

Stylish retro-camping: the only rental cars that are really suited to the romantic exploration of Jersey are the five *VW Campers* that have been beautifully decked out by a classic car restorer – they offer models from 1967 to 2009 → **p. 120**

INSIDER TIP A blond hedgehog?!

"Nightlife" means something a little different on Alderney: here, you go *hedgehogspotting*. As the sun sets, embark on a hunt for some of the 1,000 or so hedgehogs with light-coloured prickles that live on the island. Grab a torch and get looking for these rare blond beauties → **p. 86**

INSIDER TIP Camping at the zoo

The only way to go "glamping" (glamorous camping) on Jersey is to spend the night in a roomy tent of the *Durrell Wildlife Camp* on the edge of the island's extraordinary zoo. The animals' night-time calls will make you feel you're in Africa or Madagascar → **p. 43**

INSIDER TIP Spring flowers
A fairy-tale sea of bluebells spreads beneath your feet when you go for a spring stroll through the *Bluebell Wood* south of Guernsey's St Peter Port → p. 73

INSIDER TIP Calories with coloratur
Grand cinema, *Ruby's* restaurant in St Helier: the staff can sing, act and the service reflects this. The style is Art Deco, so you can also dress in style → p. 54

INSIDER TIP Fast food, enjoyed slowly
The *Braye Chippy* on Alderney serves fish and chips with a slow food ethos: the fish is caught right next to chip shop's own front door → p. 85

INSIDER TIP Loads of cash
70,000 silver coins from Caesar's days: two Jerseymen with insider knowledge discovered the *Celtic treasure of La Hougue Bie* → p. 57

INSIDER TIP Batman's bedroom
What does a bat do when it has a bad dream? In Jersey's *Zoo*, despite the strong smell, it's difficult to leave behind the tête-à-tête with the aerial acrobats → p. 114

INSIDER TIP Vegan chic
Ethically correct style at *Little Ginger en Provence* in St Peter Port specialises in fair trade, vegan fashion and vegan accessories → p. 78

INSIDER TIP Bathe like Venus herself
To sample the refreshing pleasures of the *Venus Pool*, cross Sark and travel down to the southernmost point of the Little Sark peninsula → p. 93

INSIDER TIP Afternoon tea in a cottage garden
Teatime in a private cottage garden – Sark's green oases are open to visitors in the summer on occasion of the *Garden Walks* (photo below) → p. 96

BEST OF ...

GREAT PLACES FOR FREE
Discover new places and save money

FOR FREE

● *Splash in the sea pool!*
This round pool was built in Jersey's *Havre des Pas* in 1890 to allow people to swim no matter what the tides were doing at the time. Today, the pool still lets you swim in seawater, even when the sea itself has vanished. It's free and very popular! → p. 114

● *Orchid show for free*
From about mid-May to mid-June on the wildflower meadow *Le Noir Pré* in Jersey's St Ouen's Bay 60,000 fabulous wild orchids are in bloom. During the last week of May, the National Trust offers free guided walking tours → p. 36

● *Beautiful mussel-covered chapel*
Covered in mussels, the lovingly created *Little Chapel* on Guernsey is an unusual attraction that costs nothing to visit. It's the last stop on a Way of the Cross pilgrimage walk that invites you to meditate in idyllic natural surroundings (Photo) → p. 61

● *St Peter Port from above*
The key to the triumphal tower can be obtained for half an hour from Guernsey's art museum. The structure offers the most magnificent view of the most magnificent town in the Channel. You have to pay for museum entry, but the *Victoria Tower* is free → p. 76

● *Catch your own meal*
Are you staying in self-catering accommodation? Then do as the islanders do: catch your dinner from the long walkway on St Catherine's Breakwater! → p. 44

● *Birds instead of bombs*
The Nazis forced concentration camp prisoners to cover Alderney in concrete observation bunkers. It's not soldiers who look through the observation slits of the *Wildlife Trust Bunker* today, however: bird lovers use Alderney's fortifications to observe the flight manoeuvres of puffins and gannets → p. 85

●●●● Dots in guidebook refer to "Best of ..." tips

ONLY ON THE CHANNEL ISLANDS
Unique experiences

● *Five gardens of Eden*
Subtropical plants can grow in the Channel Islands thanks to the warming effect of the Gulf Stream and the islanders' green fingers. *Judith Quérée's* Jersey garden of herbaceous perennials is a real oasis → p. 35

● *Mudflat hiking*
The south of Jersey is so flat that the sea retreats far from the coast at low tide before flooding back at speed later on. When the sea's out, you can walk over the seemingly infinite mudflats towards France and up to the spooky *Seymour Tower*, where you can even spend the night → p. 55

● *Six weeks of feasting*
For six weeks in the autumn, the islands are transformed into a gourmet's paradise. You can dine like a French king during the *Tennerfest*, when nearly 200 restaurants, pubs and cafés on Jersey and Guernsey offer multi-course menus from £10 to £20 → p. 29

● *Vegetables to go*
Hedge Veg is the name for the tomatoes, potatoes, apples, pears, cherries and cut flowers that are offered for sale along the hedgerows of the islands. An honesty box (photo) stands next to each crate of vegetables. One place to find hedge veg is at the *Classic Farm Shop* on Jersey → p. 36

● *Spend your afternoon in style*
Although the food on the Channel Islands is heavily influenced by French cuisine, no afternoon would be complete without a relaxed cream tea, complete with rich cream from the islands' cows. It's a very British part of island life. Enjoy a very inexpensive tea at *The Hungry Man* in Jersey's Rozel Bay → p. 27 and 40

● *German military architecture*
The Romans once fortified these islands, and Hitler also used them as a brick in the Atlantic Wall. The Nazis' concrete military structures still stand today. Built in a style between Bauhaus and Art Deco, Guernsey's *Pleinmont Tower* is a particularly striking example → p. 66

BEST OF ...

AND IF IT RAINS?
Activities to brighten your day

● *An impressive war museum*
It's hard to find a more successful war museum than *Jersey War Tunnels,* which brings the oppressive atmosphere of the old Nazi tunnels to life. It sounds a paradoxical idea, but it makes museum learning exciting. You'll almost be hoping for a couple of hours of rain (photo) → **p. 47**

● *Driftwood craft*
The *Fish 'n' Beads* craft workshop, set in Jersey's beautiful St Brelade's Bay, is a perfect place to sit under the porch making something from treasures combed from the beach and Tina's selection of beads. You won't care if it rains → **p. 115**

● *Country house cooking par excellence*
A perfect destination for a rainy day: who wants to try 40 types of British cheese when it's sunny outside, anyway? Every trip to Jersey should include a meal in the cosy, traditional atmosphere of the *Longueville Manor* country house hotel → **p. 54**

● *Coasteering and paddling*
If you don a neoprene suit and go sea kayaking or go walking along the steep coastal cliffs, you're going to get wet – a little bit of rain won't make a difference! → **p. 110**

● *The poet's residence*
French literary giant Victor Hugo apparently saw himself as a bit of a dab hand at interior design – the author decorated *Hauteville House*, his slightly eccentric exile residence, himself → **p. 75**

● *The big screen on a small island*
The best thing about going to see a film in Alderney's 90-seat cinema is that you have time to enjoy a beer in the pub opposite while they change the reels → **p. 83**

RAIN

RELAX AND CHILL OUT
Take it easy and spoil yourself

● *Ayurveda in the Channel*
Sample all the tricks and techniques of Ayurvedic massage. There's also meditation, baths and treatments – even for men. Jersey's *Ayush Wellness Spa* is one of the first of its kind in Great Britain → p. 55

● *Panoramic lounge*
The view from the fifth floor of the *Corbière Radio Tower* over St Ouen's Bay and the Corbière Lighthouse is unbeatable. Boasting 360-degree windows, this is Jersey's highest place to relax → p. 52

● *The scent of lavender*
Is there anything more relaxing than sitting in the café at *Jersey Lavender*, looking out over the beautiful garden, and sipping a glass of champagne with a sprig of lavender? → p. 47

● *A picturesque bay*
Relax in style and enjoy the panoramic view from this beautiful spot. You won't be the first: Auguste Renoir once lingered here for weeks, painting the view of Guernsey's *Moulin Huet bay* (photo) → p. 63

● *A coach ride on Sark*
You won't see a single car if you take a cosy, 90-minute *coach trip* around both parts of the island. The horses even keep calm when riding over the high La Coupée land bridge → p. 96

● *A window on the coast*
Take a stroll through the Seigneur of Sark's magnificent gardens before walking down to enjoy a panoramic view of the coast through the naturally formed *Window in the Rock* → p. 94

● *Luxury camping on the edge of wilderness*
It's fantastic that there is a zoo on Jersey with gorillas and lemurs. But the "glamping" option on the edge of the park in luxury safari tents makes it even better. You can sip a glass of wine in the evening and listen to the animal sounds in the darkness!
→ p. 43

INTRODUCTION

DISCOVER THE CHANNEL ISLANDS!

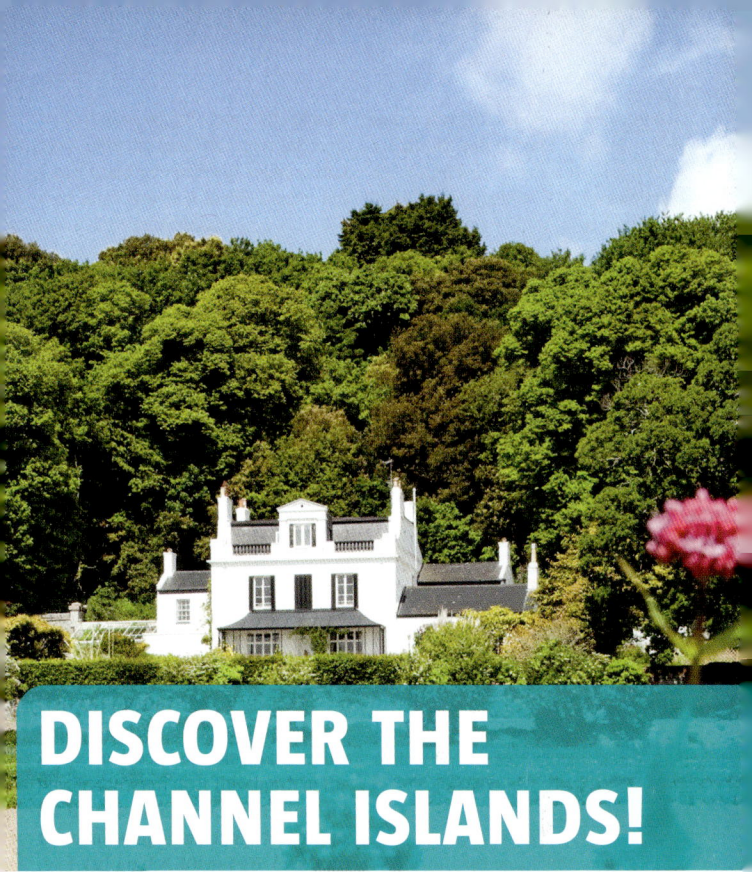

When the tide is out, it looks as if someone has pulled a plug out of the Channel between England and France. The beautiful island of Jersey is left *high and dry* and grows by more than a third in size. Fishing boats and yachts lie at odd angles on the sandy seabed. One marine biologist who leads tours over the mudflats poetically calls this extra bit of land Jersey's "better half": "Thanks to the shallow seabed around the island and the twelve-metre tidal range, nature gives us a temporary gift twice a day." Guernsey, the second largest Channel Island, enjoys the same transformation. Jersey, Guernsey, Alderney, Sark and Herm: five islands with five different characters. The Channel Islands – charming oases with a *mild, Gulf Stream climate* – aren't just attractive for wealthy individuals looking to stash away their money. It has great beaches, gardens filled with subtropical plants, cliff-tops covered in wild flowers. The islanders speak like the English and eat like the French. Between meals, the *coastal paths* offer beautiful views for walkers, and cyclists enjoy priority in the labyrinth of narrow, winding lanes and ruettes tranquilles in the islands' heartlands.

"A piece of France that fell into the sea and was gathered up by England." That's how French novelist Victor Hugo, who lived in exile here in the 19th century, gazing out

Photo: St Aubin on Jersey

High seas: a storm is brewing on the jetty in St Peter Port harbour

to France in good weather, once described the small archipelago. Today, the Channel Islands blends French *savoir-vivre with British eccentricity*, a French passion for seafood with a Victorian love of gardens – it's one of the most agreeable cultural combinations in Europe today.

The five islands are huddled together in the Gulf of Saint Malo. Separated from Normandy's Cotentin peninsula around 8,000 years ago, they were once known as the Norman Islands. Geographically speaking, they're closer to France – Alderney is just 13 km/8.1 mi away from La Grande République, while 90 km/55.9 mi of sea separate it from England's south coast.

c. 4000 BC
Passage graves bear witness to the first settlements

50 BC
The Romans occupy and use the islands as a trading post

from AD 538
Christianisation

1066
William the Conqueror wins the Battle of Hastings, and the Channel Islands fall to the Anglo-Norman kingdom

1852
Victor Hugo seeks exile on Jersey and, from 1855, Guernsey

1883
Auguste Renoir visits, creating sketches and 18 works in oil

INTRODUCTION

In wartime, the archipelago was often a strategic bone of contention or bridgehead. Nowadays, peaceful *cultural and linguistic characteristics* coexist; the French names on road signs and houses are often pronounced with an English accent. The *abundant flora* comes from all over the world, which is why you sometimes feel like you are in the Mediterranean, in the Canaries or New Zealand – it's all due to the Gulf Stream. Even politically, the islands are legendary. The Channel Islands – altogether they cover 77 mi^2 – are a crown territory of the English monarch. Parliaments and laws govern modern island life, although some customs are said to be ancient. The States of Jersey and Guernsey are also regarded as important offshore tax havens.

The islands have had a turbulent past. Evidence of the *German occupation* during Second World War is still visible. The Germans installed 17 million ft^3 of reinforced concrete on the islands, barricading themselves in. They christened Guernsey, Jersey and Alderney Gustav, Jakob and Abel to make their names easier for Germans to say. Networks of concrete tunnels, bunker complexes, *forts and watchtowers* stand as reminders of this time. Many have been converted into museums and memorials. These fortifications stand in stark contrast to the islands' enchanting scenery – a stunning natural backdrop of *steep cliffs*, the second highest tidal range in the world, *footpaths overgrown with broom*,

> **The mild Gulf Stream allows 1,500 plant varieties to thrive**

1935–1939 First air connections to the Islands

1940 German troops occupy the islands

1945 The islands are freed from the German occupation

1973 After Great Britain's signs up to the EEC, the islands join the EU's free trade area

2008 The first democratic elections take place on Sark

2021 Island Games on Guernsey with 14 Olympic sports and 3,000 athletes from the Islands

fine sandy beaches, carpets of flowers, and a deep turquoise sea. Daffodils grow on the edges of beaches, *hydrangeas* blossom in the gardens, and mimosas, camellias and roses climb elegantly over old stone walls. The architecture is quintessentially British: imposing Victorian and Tudor-style *mansions* hide behind boxwood hedges; brick-coloured farmhouses dot the islands' heartlands, which are criss-crossed by narrow roads that test the nerves of drivers.

Each of the five islands is slice of paradise. Jersey, the largest island at 46 mi^2 is home to around 100,000 inhabitants. The view from the air is of white greenhouses spanning whole fields, pastures and gardens separated by clean, ruler-straight lines, and blue swimming pools peppering the park-like grounds of large villas.

> **Broom covered cliff-top paths, sandy beaches and carpets of flowers**

Daily life in these elite island kingdoms can be *rather eccentric*: one story tells of a collector who built a transparent floor in his castle just so that he could look at his collection of classic cars ...

Numerous banking institutions can be found in the lanes of the small capitals. The Channel Islands are a popular tax haven, with the same fiscal status as Monaco and Liechtenstein. Finance has replaced tourism and agriculture as the islands' most important source of income, and now represents a good half of the archipelago's revenue.

You'll constantly stumble across traces of ancient cultures. When a cave was discovered in Jersey's St Brelade's bay in 1968, even Prince Charles got digging with a spade to extract the prehistoric mammoth and rhinoceros bones from the ground. The first settlers on Jersey had driven the animals over the cliffs – an effective hunting method from the days before gunpowder.

Menhirs, dolmen and passage tombs are numerous. Some of these magical places were created as long ago as 3500 BC. The Le Déhus passage tomb on Guernsey provides a real puzzle for researchers: was it, for instance, a site of ritual burial? There are many remaining mysteries in this small *fairy-tale world*, the second largest Channel Island at 24 mi^2. Guernsey has the Channel's most striking capital – St Peter Port, but its interior is also well worth a visit. Gardens filled with rhubarb and white valerian ramble down to the sea. *Hunchbacked stone cottages* with camellias growing out front would make a great setting for a murder mystery.

If you've walked over Guernsey's cliff-top paths and drifted by boat through bays that once inspired the artist Auguste Renoir, then it's time for your very own Robinson Crusoe adventure. Herm, the smallest Channel Island at just 0.8 mi^2, situated just 20 minutes from Guernsey by ferry, is a *beach paradise*. You'll find pure relaxation

INTRODUCTION

there on Caribbean-style beaches and in classy hotels, apartments and cottages. With no cars, noise or air pollution, it's a perfect *retreat* from city life.

Sark is entirely different. The 1.9-mi^2 small, high plateau with a fantastic rocky coastline has only been inhabited since the 16th century and has its own head who is

You constantly come across Stone Age megalithic burial sites like Le Déhus on Guernsey

known as a Seigneur – a lord under the Queen. Since two billionaires settled on a neighbouring island in the early 2000s, Sark was obliged to keep step with the times and embrace democratic rules. However, only *horse-drawn vehicles*, tractors and bicycles are still permitted on the island and there is no street-lighting at night to interfere with the starlit sky. The fifth island in the group is rather surprising:

The eccentric lives of the island's elite

Alderney. The northernmost dwarf island has a much harsher climate and few flowering plants grow here. The character of Alderney (covering an area of 3.1 mi^2) is influenced by century-old ramparts.

Coastal hikers can envisage dramatic film scenarios and the friendly *screeching of sea birds*. The residents here are trying to get away from things, so the saying goes: from their wife, the taxman or the world. Weekend visitors like spending the day on the beach and going to the *pubs* in the evening. If you have visited the Channel Islands once, you are likely to return again at some point. Nowhere else in Europe is it possible to escape from modern life so wonderfully.

WHAT'S HOT

1 Active islands

Body training Tidal rhythms are infectious: the islanders are just as motivated to get active. Beach yoga and SUP yoga on Jersey *(www.jersey.com/kula-yoga-jersey, www.jersey.com/yoga-in-jersey)* are also popular with visitors as well as retreat activities at Kempt Tower *(www.driftretreat.co.uk)*. Park running is another popular sport with the islanders. Everyone is welcome on the 5-km (3.1-mi) courses across L'Ancresse common on Guernsey *(www.parkrun.org.uk/guernsey)* and at Jersey's St Brelade's Bay.

Glowing skies 2

Stargazing The smaller the island, the less disruptive the light pollution at night. Islanders on Sark and Alderney love stargazing and they're good at it. On Sark, the Sark Astronomy Society has built its own observatory. On Alderney, the locals meet up for stargazing parties. You can often see the "green glow" at sunset.

At one with nature

3

Environment Helping *Beachwatch* 🌿 tidy up the beaches is a real event *(mcsuk.org/beachwatch/greatbritishbeachclean / photo)*. Instead of staying in a B&B, you get to camp out in the natural surroundings you've helped clean – in a tipi, for example, with a fire and a meal you've collected yourself. These trips are organised by 🌿 *Wild Guernsey* (wildguernsey.wordpress.com/wild-camping). The outdoor guides are committed to Guernsey's natural environment and offer Wild *Food Workshops* with foraging tours to collect and prepare plants from the seashore and forest – a good opportunity to get to know some islanders.

There are lots of new things to discover on the Channel Islands. A few of the most interesting are listed below

Folk around the clock

Island sounds For several years, young musicians have been discovering folk music in the most remote island living rooms and barns. The popular band, The Recks, from Sark are into "schizophrenic folk" *(www.the recks.co.uk)*. Cosmic Fish is also hugely popular. Guernsey, Herm and Sark especially have a lively music scene that rivals the larger island of Jersey. The festival Vale Earth Fair *(www.vale earthfair.org)* attracts all the islands' pop, rock and folk fans. Weekly news updates are broadcast on BBC stations for Guernsey and Jersey. Even the Mermaid Tavern (photo) on the tiny island of Herm is now a popular stage. Check the website for the latest updates: *www.guernseygigs.com*

Up and away

Climbing With such fantastic rocky coastlines, it was only a question of time before the Channel Islands attracted climbing fanatics. If you want to climb in company, get down to the *Jersey Rock Climbing Club (www.jersey climbs.com)*. In winter, they meet in the Langford Sports Centre in St Saviour. Bouldering is also popular thanks to the variety of routes to choose from. You can scramble over the cliffs, quay walls and the tiny islands that are revealed when the tide goes out. The *Guernsey Mountaineering Club (www.gmc.org.gg)* can help you find a suitable bouldering spot – they have detailed information online. *Pinnacle Sports (10 Highfield Estate | St Helier)* can sort you out with all the equipment you need.

IN A NUTSHELL

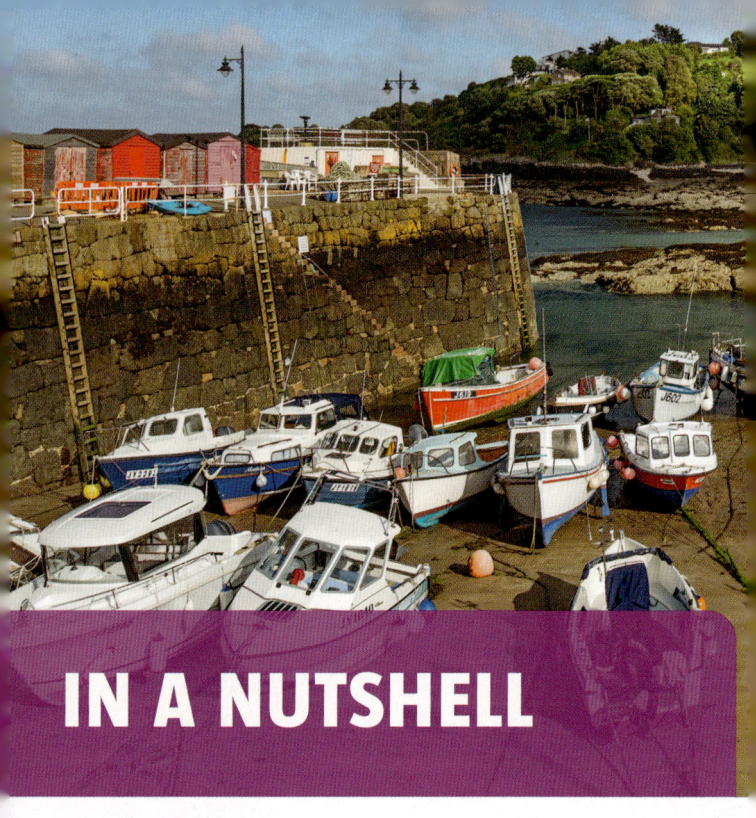

CHANNEL BREXIT

Brexit? Which Brexit? The islands can feel rather on the sunny side of the future EU without Great Britain because they are crown territory but not part of the EU. The islands have their own EU protocol, especially in relation to trading goods. Financial trading with London's banks – not always fully transparent – will continue to function somehow and migrant workers from Portugal and Poland will be resident islanders, even if they are at the back of the queue on the luxurious property market. Some expert thinktanks even consider the islands' special deal with the EU as the best blueprint for Great Britain. That would then be a "soft Brexit", which could be called a "Channel Brexit". Islands simply have to be inventive to survive – and they're well practised at this.

TREACHEROUS WATERS

Swimming in the Channel isn't like taking a bath. In the summer, bathers have to make do with maximum water temperatures of 17–19 °C/62.6–66.2 °F. And the water doesn't like to stay in one place for too long: the tide goes out twice a day, and with a tidal range of 10–12 m/32.8–39.4 ft there are only very specific times you can swim each day. It also places the islands' landscape in a permanent and dramatic state of flux. Jersey flattens out towards the south and gains an extra 40 per cent in size at low tide. The island also rises and falls

Martello towers and German military bunkers are testaments to the island's turbulent past

by around 5 cm/2 in with each turn of the tide thanks to the power of the water pressure involved. Bays and wide sandy beaches come and go, making them potentially dangerous, especially for beach walkers and cavers. Yachts lie stranded on the dry seabed for hours, while fishing boats are pulled high up the beach on tractors and parked on the house-high sea walls. Speeds of up to 12 knots have been measured in the currents off Alderney, meaning that yacht and motor launch sailors need to be extremely careful when sailing in this part of the Channel. And they're not the only ones: the waters of the Gulf of Saint Malo, off the coast of France, are also treacherous for shipping. The islanders used to profit from the regular shipwrecks by "wrecking" – picking the spilled cargo off the rocks. Ancient wrecks are still being discovered in the waters off the islands.

GERMAN CONCRETE

The islands' airports had been operational for only a few years when the

21

Jersey cow: the cream of the crop

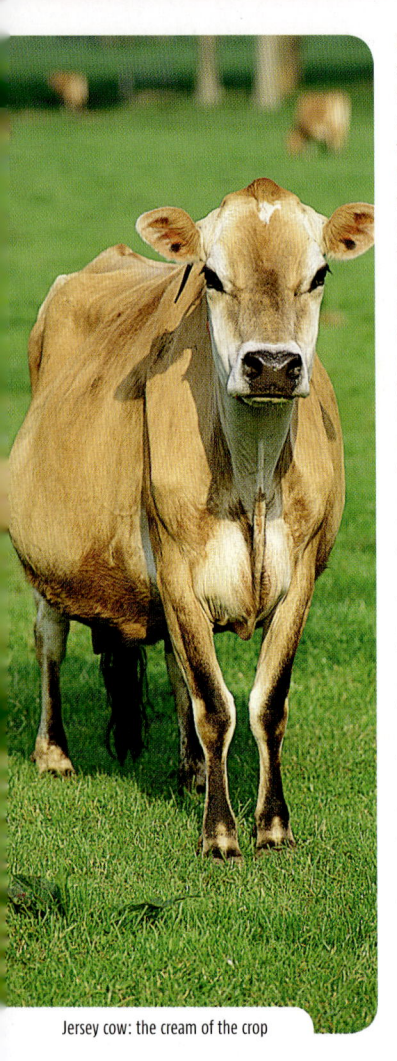

German Luftwaffe landed on the archipelago between the 30 June and the 3 July 1940. Thousands of islanders, especially children, had been evacuated a few days previously. Initially, the German invaders bombed potato trucks and killed a few civilians, just to make sure that the islanders weren't able to defend themselves. On 1 July, a pilot climbed out of his plane, walked to the telegraph office, and phoned the Bailiff – an island dignitary – to tell him that the islands were being occupied. The Germans stayed for almost five years and branded the islands – the only bit of English territory they succeeded in conquering – with a mark that is still visible today in the many military installations. Place names were Germanised, German street signs were put up, and the Wochenschau – a weekly German news bulletin – became a fixture in cinemas. Despite censoring the island newspaper, islanders managed to send coded messages by printing strategically placed spelling mistakes. The people coped the best they could, collaborated a little to survive, and suffered a new blow when 2,000 English inhabitants were deported to the south of Germany at the end of 1942.

The arrival of Hitler's building division and thousands of forced labourers made the deepest incision into island life. Concrete walls, tunnels, towers and bunkers were built, leading to the death of many Central European, Slavic and African workers in the process. The SS set up three work camps – named Helgoland, Borkum and Noderney – on the island of Alderney, which by then was deserted. In the end, the British never attacked their own islands and the war passed them by. The occupiers allowed the islands to continue their own administration. On 9 May 1945, they surrendered without fighting and the dreadful curse was over. This date is celebrated today as Liberation Day.

INCUBATORS IN THE ENGLISH CHANNEL

Nature in full bloom! From as early as April the wildflowers are at their best,

IN A NUTSHELL

covering the cliffs and fields with ever-changing carpets of colour right through until autumn. The coast is the first to burst into flower, followed by the hedgerows and the gardens of the islands' interior. Azaleas, hyacinths, primulas, orchids, blackthorn, roses, hydrangeas and many more besides combine to create a landscape that looks like an exquisite impressionist painting. Particularly outstanding are the palm-like cabbage trees (coryline australis), a specimen from New Zealand that also grows on England's southwest coast. The brightly coloured flowers of ice plants from South Africa, the Canary Islands, and Cape Verde are among the other interesting exotic blooms; delicate and less prominent are the orchids that flourish in May on Le Noir Pré, a former potato field in the middle of the St Ouen's Bay dunes. You should also look out for the deep-purple Jersey Orchid.

Sea birds float above this floral scene. Gulls of all varieties, gannets, cormorants and even a couple of hundred puffin arrive to nest on the islands from the middle of May. Songbirds such as the Dartford Warbler and the Stone Chat flit around in the compact woodlands of Jersey's tiny plateau and in the islands' private gardens. Make sure you take a field guide and some binoculars with you if you want to spot birds, but don't get a shock if you suddenly see a brown giant looming in front of your lens. It will be one of the beautiful Jersey or Guernsey cows that produce the high-fat milk (up to 7 per cent!) that's used to make the islands' signature yellow cream and delicious ice cream.

SLAND LINGO

Parlez-vous English? Plenty of tongue-twisters have become common parlance in the individual island languages. For historical reasons, the islanders switched from English to French and back again over the last 1,000 years. Norman

FOR BOOKWORMS AND FILM BUFFS

Mr Pye – A 1953 novel by Mervyn Peake that tells the story of a man who goes to Sark on an evangelical mission. A Channel 4 mini series adaptation was filmed in four 50-minute episodes in 1986. Shot on the island of Sark itself, the production starred Sir Derek Jacobi in the title role

Bergerac – John Nettles played a drunken, limping Jersey policeman in this BBC production that lasted for nine series in the 1980s. The cult detective's car – a 1947 Triumph Roadster – can be seen today at the Jersey Goldsmith Jewellers in St Lawrence

The Others – Nicole Kidman stars in Alejandro Amenábar's 2001 horror blockbuster about a woman living in post-war Jersey who becomes convinced that her house is haunted. The island itself starred as the film's backdrop

The Guernsey Literary and Potato Peel Pie Society – Mike Newell's 2018 film version is based on the novel of the same name by the American Mary Ann Shaffer. It is about the correspondence between a writer and a Guernsey farmer in the 1940s. It was filmed on the English south coast and on Guernsey

French, a form of *patois*, was the lingua franca on the islands for a long time. The language rolled off the tongue a little differently on each island, which is how the various dialects came into being. Many of the town and farm names on the islands are still in French, but you wouldn't know to hear it, because the names are pronounced with an English inflection. You can listen to a recording of original dialects in the Jersey Museum. Around two per cent of the islanders still speak Jèrriais or Gernesiais.

THE ISLAND AMBASSADORS

Tourism is rarely so exclusive as on the Channel Islands. Britons used to follow the reputation of the familiar Côte d'Azur with its attractive coast and hint of French ambience. Then, the big money flowed in and they left the visitors and infrastructure to their own devices. That was not such a bad idea for those who dislike overcrowding, as the coast and cuisine are still there. Now, the islanders give discerning visitors a warm, personal welcome. Tours on Alderney or Guernsey are appealing, but Jersey's new idea is quite charming: about a dozen, specially trained island ambassadors look after the guests. A channel swimmer explains the tides, a shepherd gives a guide to the north coast and Jacob sheep, a fish chef explains the difference between lobster and spider crabs. If you meet all the ambassadors you get to know the island and local people better than the fellow countrymen!

OYSTERS WITH POTATOES

They are genuine Channel Island oysters: absolutely delicious. Breeding oysters is a success in the English Channel because the rough tides with a tidal range of up to 12 m/39.4 ft ensure that the water stays clear. Off Jersey and Herm, oysters are bred from the size of a fingernail to full-bodied shellfish – and tonnes of them are exported to France. The delicacy makes an appetizing snack on the island markets where it costs less than a pound – fast food Channel Islands style. The small, early Jersey Royal potatoes make a great side dish, and tonnes of them are also exported!

TOWERS IN THE BATTLE

The islands have a great number of fortifications. Alderney in particular is full of Victorian forts and German bunkers. More romantic are the Martello towers, which stand proud all along the coasts. In the late 18th century, these squat, fortified towers with thick walls provided the best method of defending vulnerable coasts. The English forces decided to adopt such towers after almost losing a battle against soldiers stationed in such a tower at the Punta Martello on Corsica in 1794, even though the British had two warships at their disposal. The British decided to employ the same design to protect their territories around the world, including the Channel Islands. Similar fortifications had been built on the islands' coasts many years before in order to protect them from French invasion. Precursors to the Martello towers had shooting slits around the outside walls and cannons positioned on the roof. Pulling up the ladder transformed the towers into almost unconquerable targets for would-be attackers.

TAX HAVENS CALL SOS

If you're flying to the Channel Islands from London, you'll soon notice the large number of besuited office workers getting on the plane. These pas-

IN A NUTSHELL

sengers, who easily outnumber the tourists, have a very specific interest in the islands – finance. Since the 1960s, the Channel Islands have been one of the world's most popular tax havens, encouraging wealthy individuals from all over the world to bank on the islands, and many companies to shelter profits here and avoid tax. The money was discreetly managed behind closed doors, and on Jersey alone the shiny name plaques revealed the identities of almost 80 banks in those days.

The islands could only devise the fantastic money trade because their tax regimes are independent form Great Britain and the EU. Foreign businesses and corrupt powers paid no taxes on their deposits, local financial services only pay 20 per cent – the sheer volume of tax-avoiding money poured billions into the coffers. Agriculture and tourism were arrogantly neglected. After the financial crash, the EU cracked down and demanded the same tax regime for foreign and local businesses. Banks and investment funds have since moved away from the islands; islanders are losing their jobs and suddenly the gap between rich and poor is obvious. Jersey introduced a five per cent value added tax rate, Guernsey increased taxes for its citizens. A fear of bankruptcy swept the islands. A potential, but overlooked countermeasure was to make tourism a priority again and not an insider secret!

Round case: Martello towers like this one on Guernsey's north coast are everywhere

FOOD & DRINK

The tidal location makes the islands with the delicious potatoes and cream a land of plenty – the same goes for under water: all kinds of seafood thrive here. Plenty of seafood is harvested by hand – it couldn't be fresher.

Lovers of fish and seafood won't be presented with many plates of wan-looking fish and chips in the Channel Islands – instead, they'll be treated to oysters, lobster and *scallops*, which are sold to the restaurants by the basketful. A good place to start is the Parisian-style market hall in St Helier, Jersey's capital. Afterwards seek out one of the many fine restaurants dotted all over the islands. Jersey has two restaurants with *Michelin stars*: the *Bohemia* and the *Ormer*, both in St Helier. And the chefs may not be famous for their cuisine alone – one or two of the more eccentric personalities, for example, dive to collect the seafood themselves.

The archipelago's culinary day starts rather less unusually. Most of the Channel Islands' hotels offer a mix of menus to kick-start the morning: a continental breakfast with toast, jam and eggs is usually served alongside a traditional British breakfast of sausages, mushrooms, *bacon and eggs cooked in various styles.*

To really get into the island lifestyle, have a light lunch at midday. Stop off between noon and 2pm–2.30pm for a *crab pastry* or a plate with four scallops in one of the islands' brassieres, bars and bistros. Restaurants offer good-

Photo: Scones with whipped cream and berries

Haute cuisine and cream tea with scones: the islands' cooking is a fusion of French gastronomy and British tradition

value lunches – often served as business meals. The relaxed atmosphere is almost Mediterranean, with carefree diners laughing and swapping stories across the tables.

The afternoon is a time of *culinary leisure*: make sure you enjoy a ● cream tea. Taking tea every day is a great way to discover the best hotels without spending a huge amount of money. Among the top places to try are the terrace of the Sommerville hotel, looking out over St Aubin; the Atlantic hotel overlooking St Ouen's Bay in the south; and the *enchanted garden atmosphere* of the Château La Chaire in Rozel Bay. There are also many tearooms serving cream tea – try the one at St Brelade's Jersey Lavender Farm. Although heated debates rage in the southern English counties of Devon and Cornwall over how best to enjoy these treats – cream or jam on the top? – all that matters here is that the *cream* comes from Jersey or Guernsey cows. While the only fitting accompaniment to cream

27

LOCAL SPECIALITIES

bean crock/Guernsey bean jar – a stew made from vegetables, beans, onions, carrots and meat
black butter – a spicy conserve made from cooked apples
chancre crab – crabs are an island speciality. They're sublime in pastries, and make for a delicious crab salad (photo right)
cider – the fizzy apple wine was once produced everywhere on the islands. La Mare Wine Estate medium-dry cider is still produced
cod – once found all over the world, it's now highly endangered. It's not rare on the islands – yet! – and can even be found at snack bars
cream – cream from Jersey and Guernsey cows has high fat content (five to seven per cent) and protein (four per cent); it has a vanilla yellow colour and almost a nutty flavour. It is used to make ice cream and cheese and for chocolates on Sark
cream tea – a pot of tea and one or two scones, enjoyed in classic style with cream from the islands' cows and – to top it all – strawberry jam
gache melee – traditional Guernsey apple cake, served warm with cream
Jersey royal potato – a famous small potato variety, treated with seaweed as fertiliser, harvested on demand, and always freshly served
lobster – you'll seldom find lobster better than this. It's particularly well prepared on Sark
oysters – they are cultivated on the islands, exported and served everywhere. You can find them offshore on Jersey
scallops – the fleshy scallops are often eaten as a starter (photo left)
turbot – farmed in a German bunker and served with Jersey royals

is a fruit-packed strawberry jam, there is normally a choice of tea – *Earl Grey*, Ceylon blend or Assam tea – poured from silver pots into wafer-thin bone china. Business people and bankers celebrate the end of the working day from 5pm, often meeting in St Peter Port and St Helier for champagne and *cocktails* in the bistros and bars.
During the evening, you could either head to a pub for a cosy meal – the fare ranges from *British roast beef* or lasagne to the day's catch of lobster – or meet for dinner between 6pm and 8.30pm

FOOD & DRINK

(sometimes later). In pubs, it's normal to order and pay at the bar.

While ordering dinner in hotels is a beautifully orchestrated process – the menu is introduced to you while you're sipping an *aperitif in the bar* – in restaurants it is usual for you to be shown straight to a table. There, French-influenced gourmet cuisine is generally the order of the day, though British favourites often feature too. Why not start off with *fresh oysters* or the smoked duck breast? Then perhaps order a piece of lamb in a rosemary jus, before sampling a very British treat – *freshly baked apple pie* with cream or vanilla ice cream. The whole experience is the result of a culinary alliance between England and France. Other influences are also evident: menus may include the elegantly spiced flavours of Thai cooking, and take inspiration from the Italian love of fresh vegetables, garlic and olive oil.

Cuisine rules especially supreme during the ● Tennerfest (www.tennerfest.com). Almost 200 restaurants, bistros and pubs take part in this *food festival* held between the start of October and the middle of November. Extremely reasonable three- (and sometimes four) course set menus are priced between £10 (a "*tenner*") and £20. Menus are shown on the website from September. You can walk off the calories in the autumnal landscape during the day before spending a *rustic evening by the fire* or going out to dine in style. The festival makes the Channel a great destination late into the year.

The very best oysters come from farms on Jersey and Guernsey. Good *lobsters* are also caught off the coast of Sark. You should also try fresh scallops and, if you can find them, ormers. These small *sea snails*, also called ear shells or abalones, can only be collected during low tide from January to April. They're rare, expensive and highly prized – this means it's a real stroke of luck indeed if you find them on the menu. In the meanwhile,

Fertilised with kelp: the Jersey Royal is the queen of the potatoes

an inventor started to grow them in the tideland. Fresh new potatoes make for a delicious accompaniment – *Jersey Royal potatoes* are prized by those in the know. A good glass of wine is the perfect way to round off the whole experience. Although French imports rule the wine lists, a home-grown Jersey variety from the *winery* La Mare Wine Estate also features. Beer is also brewed on the islands.

29

SHOPPING

You don't exactly visit the islands to go shopping, even if the prices are slightly lower than on the mainland because of the low or zero-rated VAT (on Jersey). The steep drop in the value of the pound is partly compensated by price rises. However, the designer shop windows in both island capitals take great trouble to entice shoppers. St Helier has carefully and successfully combined its Liberty Wharf mall with new architecture at an old slaughterhouse in the harbour. In St Peter Port, the atmosphere while window shopping in the steep alleyways above the harbour is almost medieval. The shops are usually open Mondays to Saturdays from 8am or 9am to 5pm or 6pm, on Guernsey some shops are also open Sundays.

JERSEY WOOL

In 1608, knitting had become so popular among Jersey's inhabitants that the island's parliament took action: they banned anyone over the age of 15 from knitting during the harvest, when all hands were needed in the fields. Anyone found breaking this law faced being whipped or imprisoned. Young and old, men and women, everyone knitted, providing England with millions of socks. The famous sweater – called a "Jersey" all over the world – is the only remnant of that once very profitable export market. Jerseys are straight cut, with a narrow waist and slim arms. It remains the garment of choice for fishermen even today: the wool stays warm in the wind and rain, is undamaged by salt water, and is moisture-resistant thanks to its fat content. Most Jerseys are blue with a ribbed stitch at the top of the sleeve and an anchor on the chest. Guernsey pullovers don't have the anchor.

JEWELLERY

Catherine Best *(www.catherinebest.com)* on Guernsey has won numerous design prizes for her limited-edition jewellery. She also likes to use little-known precious stones. You can find one of her showrooms in the *Windmill* in St Peter Port. *Jersey Pearl's* elegant sales rooms *(www.jerseypearl.com)*, situated on the northernmost end of Five Mile Road in the west of Jersey, are worth visiting. A family-run business, it sells authentic pearl jewellery and beautiful imitations. It's open ev-

Island shopping: choose between maritime accessories, creamy chocolates, woollen knitwear and delicious pralines

ery day and can be reached by bus. Another long-standing family business is *Jersey Goldsmiths* in St Helier's Queen Street. It sells a wide selection of handmade pieces incorporating precious stones. The jewellery set with polished coloured granite is also very interesting. It's worth visiting their showrooms, even if you're not looking to buy.

SOUVENIRS

Small island knickknacks such as postage stamps and beer mats make for pretty holiday souvenirs, even if you aren't a true collector. All of the Channel Islands print their own beautiful – and occasionally eccentric – postage stamps *(www.guernseystamps.com)*. Alderney's own versions, decorated with floral and animal motifs, are particularly attractive. More bizarre are the medals of the German army or their marching albums that you can purchase in La Valette Underground Military Museum near St Peter Port. Slightly less controversial souvenirs are the small, colourful shells from the wonderful Shell Beach on Herm. Here, the island honey is also certainly an attraction. And you'll remember the old pubs back home if you simply pick up a few beer mats with their attractive designs.

TASTY TREATS

Small, but rich in calories: the delicious Brie cheese made from the creamy milk of Jersey and Guernsey cows makes a tasty souvenir to take home. Local cream is also used by *Rebecca's Chocolates* on Guernsey and by *Caragh Chocolate* on Sark. *La Mare Wine Estate (www.lamarewineestate.com)* on Jersey keeps the old tradition of cider production alive. Tasty souvenirs from the estate include apple brandy, Clos de la Mare (an almost honey-like wine), jams and black butter – a conserve made from apples and herbs.

JERSEY

The largest Channel Island has the archipelago's most dramatic cliffs, a fashionable west coast, an urbane city lifestyle, and bays that pirates would be proud to call home. This microcosmic world of around 46 mi² broke away from France 8,000 years ago. Today, it lies in the Gulf Stream, 20 km/12.4 mi off the Normandy coast.

The island's 100,000-strong population – only half of whom were born here – enjoys more sun than anywhere else in Great Britain and a lot of political independence. Jersey is also one of Europe's best-known tax havens. You don't notice that you are in an offshore banking paradise outside EU borders because the headquarters of about 50 banks and companies like Apple are extremely low key on Jersey and Guernsey. Where are the 1.3 billion-plus tax-free pounds on Jersey alone? Only the many financiers in their suits are dressed smartly. Bling? There's no sign of it.

This financial wealth remains discreet. Goodness knows who's living behind the island's granite walls, but you might be able to guess the size of their bank accounts from their fancy cars. Such sleek and sporty models hardly get beyond second gear, however, because it's rare to reach the 64 km/h/40 mph limit on the island roads. On the narrow green lanes – country roads where cyclists, pedestrians and horse riders have right of way – the limit is just 24 km/h/15 mph.

Leisurely explorers will still come across the famous Jersey cows. Their

Photo: Portelet Bay

The whole world in miniature: cool Californian-style beaches, lemurs from Madagascar, Asian seafood and a Mediterranean climate

creamy milk used to be the main source of income for many islanders, but nowadays agriculture represents hardly 2 per cent of Jersey's gross national income.

The natural treasures of the coasts with strong tides protects Jersey almost on all sides as a national park. Inside the park, it's peaceful and wonderfully wild. If you feel isolated, then carry on exploring until you see the church tower of one of the twelve island villages. St Helier – with the fictional money – already feels like a city. This is why this chapter is organised according to the points on the compass, travelling in a clockwise direction from the west. St Helier is covered at the end of this chapter.

THE WEST

The island's landscape – which seems winding, rural and small elsewhere – really opens up on the west coast along St Ouen's Bay.

THE WEST

Only accessible at low tide: Corbière Lighthouse on south-west Jersey

Behind the beach, which stretches for an impressive 7 km/4.4 mi, lie the undulating dunes of Les Mielles, created by the incoming westerly wind. During Second World War, the Germans fortified the bay with concrete walls and laid mines on the beach, fearing that the open nature of the bay made it vulnerable to a British attack. This, along with the area's isolation from the post-war architectural development evident in other parts of Jersey, allowed a rich flora to develop here; it is now protected by Jersey's National Trust. The nature reserve swarms with nesting birds in the summer – St Ouen's Pond is a particularly rich avian hotspot – and migratory birds stop over in spring and autumn. 17 types of seriously endangered animals also live here. Entry is free, and a German bunker serves as a bird hide. Among the often seen birds here are moorhens, skylarks, cuckoos, teals, sand martins, lapwings and owls. Between mid-May and mid-June numerous orchids bloom, and botanists can find up to 400 types of plant along the footpaths in the dunes. Three golf courses are the coast's concession to fine living.

Just a few hundred feet from the secluded dunes and the bird paradise of St Ouen's Pond, you'll find a contrasting scene of ocean living: cool surfers watch the breakers from the terraces of the cafés and lend the otherwise well-behaved island a more bohemian feel. This impression increases when the sun goes down. A twilit walk down the beach promenade is highly recommended. The sort of show the waves and the surfers will be providing at the time depends on the variable state of the tides.

Jersey's western interior is home to the tranquil parishes of St Ouen and St Peter. St Ouen is the largest parish on the island, while St Peter has Jersey's tallest church tower (37 m/121.4 ft).

SIGHTSEEING

CORBIÈRE POINT (129 D5) (*A14*)
The view from the island's southwestern point falls on ★ *Corbière Lighthouse*, the world's first concrete lighthouse, built on a tidal island in 1874. The white tower sits in picturesque style on a red granite rock that was mined on Jersey, transported

JERSEY

5 km/3.1 mi by rail, and shipped out from St Aubin.
The rails have been replaced today by the Corbière Railway Walk, which is easily accessed on foot or by bike. You can walk to the lighthouse at low tide. The ☘ *Lighthouse Restaurant (Rue de la Corbière | tel. 01534 74 61 27 | www.corbierephare.com | Moderate)* offers a magnificent view and good food.

LA GRANDE ROUTE DES MIELLES
(129 E3–5) (*m B11–13*)
Known as "five mile road", this coastal route is the Channel Islands' answer to Hollywood's Sunset Boulevard. The drive from the south is breathtaking. It's almost the only piece of straight asphalt on Jersey, but don't speed up! The 64 km/h/40 mph limit still applies!

GROSNEZ CASTLE AND LE PINACLE ☘
(129 D1–2) (*m A9–10*)
On a fine day, Guernsey and Sark (around 25 km/15.5 mi and 18 km/11.2 mi away) look within striking distance of Grosnez Point, a rocky bluff on Jersey's northwest coast. The romantic-looking archway of the 14th-century Grosnez Castle still stands. A footpath – ideal for morning jogs and with great views – leads south over Les Landes plateau to the 61 m-/200.1 ft-high Le Pinacle rock, which looks a bit like a face in the morning sun. This ancient spot was a site of cult rituals for several millennia. Halfway along the path, you'll pass a German coastal tower. A path leads further down along the coast and ends on the northernmost point of the island's flat western edge. It's a INSIDER TIP **great hiking route** that takes about an hour.

JUDITH QUÉRÉE ★ ●
(129 F2) (*m C11*)
This hidden sandstone house has a magnificent garden stocked with 2,000 perennials from around the world, as well as a marsh garden full of lilies, vibrantly coloured roses and tree ferns. The owner,

MARCO POLO HIGHLIGHTS

★ **Corbière Lighthouse**
This spectacular lighthouse can only be reached with dry feet at low tide → p. 34

★ **St Ouen's Bay**
A wild beach and a nature reserve of rolling dunes on the west coast → p. 37

★ **St Brelade's Parish Church and Fishermen's Chapel**
A magical place with a beautiful graveyard → p. 48

★ **La Mare Wine Estate**
Wine, cider and spicy conserves → p. 40

★ **Mont Orgueil Castle**
Gorey boasts Jersey's oldest and most atmospheric castle → p. 44

★ **Longueville Manor**
Romantic island dining in an old manor house → p. 54

★ **Maritime Museum**
Everything you ever wanted to know about the sea → p. 53

★ **Durrell Wildlife Conservation Trust**
Jersey's Zoo is the hub of the Durrell Wildlife Trust's animal protection activities → p. 39

★ **Judith Quérée**
Roses, lilies and ferns: an enchanted garden full of fascinating flowers → p. 35

★ **La Hougue Bie**
A Stone Age grave, a chapel and a bunker museum → p. 57

35

THE WEST

Judith, tirelessly leads knowledgeable tours through her flourishing empire. *May–Sept by appointment. Tue–Thu 11am and 2pm | £7 | Léoville | Le Chemin des Garennes | tel. 01534 48 21 91 | www.judithqueree.com*

INSIDER TIP LE NOIR PRÉ ●
(129 E3) (*m B11–12*)

This wildflower meadow is almost a fairy-tale location on the breathtaking coast. But around 60,000 orchids bloom here in May and June. Be sure to look out for the Jersey Orchid in particular. *Chemin de L'Ouzière | www.nationaltrust.je/orchid-field-le-noir-pre*

LA ROCCO TOWER (129 D5) (*m B13*)

The round coastal tower about a mile offshore in the middle of the sea is like a dream destination. It was built around 1800 to defend against the French. It was damaged in the Second World War under fire from German occupiers. It's well worth a visit – and you can even stay overnight! With a guide, the no-frills adventure across the sand costs £350 for a group of six. *www.jerseyheritage.org/holiday*

WETLAND CENTRE (129 E3) (*m B12*)

The bird kingdom in the wetland Les Mielles is a nature reserve and can be easily observed through the windows of a dune fortress. With enthralling nature information – free of charge. *short.travel/kai32*

FOOD & DRINK

BIG VERN'S (129 E3) (*m B12*)

This beach café on the Grande Route des Mielles is very popular with the locals. Great breakfasts and tasty fish from the grill. *Daily | tel. 01534 48 17 05 | Budget–Moderate*

INSIDER TIP FAULKNER FISHERIES
(129 D2) (*m A10*)

Sean Faulkner keeps seafood and edible fish in a bunker by the sea in L'Étacq. The large crabs are real head-turners, the sauces and dressings make lovely souvenirs, and the fish is a great buy for self-caterers. If you're feeling peckish, why not try some reasonably priced oysters! *April–Oct barbecue menu Tue–Sat noon–3pm | tel. 01534 48 35 00 | www.faulknerfisheries.co.uk | Budget*

THE LINE UP (129 E4) (*m B12*)

Bacon and avocado rolls, burgers and coffee: this mobile kiosk serves nutritious, inexpensive fast food from a central location on a west coast beach. *Daily | Budget*

OCEAN ☘ (129 E5) (*m B13*)

Will Holland cooks exquisite tasting menus with a sea view. This restaurant is located in *The Atlantic* (*Expensive*), a four-star hotel on the west coast. *Daily | Le Mont de la Pulente | tel. 01534 74 41 01 | www.theatlantichotel.com | Expensive*

EL TICO (129 E4) (*m B12*)

A popular beach restaurant on the Grande Route des Mielles with very reasonably priced fish meals. The service is laid back but good. *Daily | tel. 01534 48 20 09 | Budget–Moderate*

SHOPPING

CLASSIC FARM SHOP ●
(129 F3) (*m C–D12*)

Jersey is well geared for self-catering and providing for peckish visitors between meals. ● *Hedge Veg Stalls* can be discovered all over the island. Place a small contribution in the honesty box and help yourself to some fresh fruit or vegetables – which are often marked as organic.

JERSEY

Authentic farm shops offer a larger selection and rare delicacies. In the *Manor Farm* shop, Jersey's only dairy farm in St Peter, Julia Quénault sells `INSIDER TIP` **home-made cheeses**: camembert, brie and a very tasty Jersey Golden Blue, all of which make great buys to take home. The meat from young bulls is aromatic due to the animals being fed on daffodil meadows after the flowers have been harvested. As well as all this, you can buy eggs, preserves, wines and much more besides. *La Route du Manoir | St Peter | www.classicfarmshop.com*

SURFING (129 E3–4) (*B11–13*)

The best conditions for wave riding can be found in the centre of the wide St Ouen's Bay. You can watch surfers between the El Tico and Watersplash restaurants. You can also rent boards yourself or take to the waves face down on a bodyboard. *www.jerseysurfschool.co.uk*

St Ouen's Bay: the tidal cycle in the Channel changes the face of the bay many times a day

SPORTS & ACTIVITIES

GOLF (129 E4–5) (*B12–13*)

These two 18-hole golf courses in the dunes are reminiscent of the famous coastal links in Scotland: *Les Mielles Golf and Country Club (St Ouen's Bay | www.lesmielles.com)* and *La Moye Golf Club (St Brelade | www.lamoyegolfclub.co.uk)*

BEACHES

ST OUEN'S BAY ★
(129 D–E 2–5) (*A–B 11–13*)

The rolling ocean throws itself hard against Jersey's long, wide west coast. Wave riders and windsurfers can spend whole days here enjoying the surf in the designated safe areas; swimmers should always keep within the flagged sections of the beaches that are watched over by coastguards in summer. Be aware that beaches that are usually reserved for people sometimes serve as tracks for car races at low tide. You can find burgers, coffee and car parks every couple of miles.

37

THE NORTH

ENTERTAINMENT

WATERSPLASH (129 E3–4) (*B12*)
This bar with tinted windows is populated by the flip-flop wearing members of the local surfing scene. It's an active social hub, a lounge and a diner all in one – inexpensive fish and chips are included on the menu. Come at the weekend to listen to live music ranging from folk to rock. Check out the programme and the daily surfing news on the website. A late bus will take you back to St Helier in the summer. *Daily | tel. 01534 48 28 85 | www.watersplashjersey.com*

WHERE TO STAY

ATLANTIC HOTEL (129 E5) (*B13*)
Enjoy understated luxury in one of Jersey's best hotels. There's a pool, great food, a view of the sea and a golf course. *50 rooms | Le Mont de la Pulente | St Brelade | tel. 01534 74 41 01 | www.theatlantichotel.com | Expensive*

LE DON HILTON (129 E3) (*B12*)
This solid cottage with its brick roof is one of the most unusual coastal forts on the island. The building, whitewashed today, has stood here by the coastal promenade, opposite the dunes of St Ouen's Pond, since at least 1665. The building – visible from far and wide – once served as a coastal watch, gunpowder store and canon emplacement. From 1815 to 1832, the building was inhabited by one Mary Best and her children – most of the coastal forts having become obsolete by this time. In 1975, a later owner, Colonel Hilton, presented it to the National Trust for Jersey – a society for the protection of the island's monuments and landscape. Today, the place makes a beautiful picnic spot to watch the sunset. Groups can rent the building year-round for a minimum of two days. There's a barbecue and place for rental toilets outside and space for six sleeping bags. An **INSIDER TIP** ideal stop for groups of campers, hikers and cyclists who want to explore the reasonably priced west coast and its dune land. *2 days £150 | tel. 01534 48 31 93 | www.nationaltrust.je/site/le-don-hilton*

INSIDER TIP LES ORMES VILLAGE
(129 E5) (*B14*)
The wooden bungalows in this holiday village situated in the dunes of St Ouen's Bay can house four to six people. They're in a wonderful seaside location, but a bit small. Two adults and two children cost from around £1,010 in the high season. *Tel. 01534 49 70 00 | www.lesormesjersey.co.uk*

THE NORTH

Live the high life – Jersey's landscape reaches its highest point in the north.

If you've navigated your way across the island by car or by bus, the sight of the ocean will soon persuade you to park your vehicle and take a stroll. The coast here is invigorating, an inspiration to get active and explore. Small bays are perfect lingering spots. Take a hike along the coastal path and dive through a sea of ferns – your efforts will be rewarded by a magnificent view. You run the risk of not reaching your destination any time soon – you'll constantly be tempted to sit down on a rocky outcrop in the sun or stop for a cream tea in a small bay. The descents into the small and beautiful bays and inlets are all steep with corkscrew bends; below, an ensemble of beach, fishing boats, café and bus stops await you – every two hours, it's a perfect break for coastal hikers. Even if you're staying in the busy south of the island,

JERSEY

the quiet beauty of the north is only a short bus journey away. In the northern interior, the coastline is followed at a respectful distance by a signposted main road that leads through the three parish communities of St Mary, St John and Trinity. In contrast to the name of the villages themselves, most of the street names are in French – they're often christened after the monikers of old, bygone ships.

SIGHTSEEING

DEVIL'S HOLE AND SOREL POINT
(130 A1) (*D9–10*)

A hiking trail between Devil's Hole and Sorel Point is an inviting half-day hiking tour with fabulous coastal views. The starting point is the car park of the quaint country guesthouse, the Priory Inn (also easy to reach with bus No. 7). A short detour – keep a look-out for the classical devil's sculpture in the undergrowth – leads to Devil's Hole, where the sea water rushes in and at high tide the sea spray reaches skywards. From here, the path heads in a north-easterly direction to the cliff Sorel Point with lighthouse. The granite below is dark red and glows in the setting sun. From Sorel Point, you can loop back over small roads to the Priory Inn. Here, you should order the INSIDER TIP **very reasonably priced seafood platter to share for two** with muscles, prawns and fried fish and banquet outdoors in the early evening sunshine.

DURRELL WILDLIFE CONSERVATION TRUST ★ (131 D3) (*G11*)

Jersey's answer to Noah's Ark, this internationally active foundation houses a great number of endangered animal species. Some of these animals were personally collected by the naturalist Gerald Durrell himself. Durrell, brother of the novelist Lawrence Durrell, was celebrated for his animal books. The INSIDER TIP **aye-aye**, a nocturnal creature, is unlikely to be seen by anyone visiting its home-

The coast by Devil's Hole: watch the Atlantic flex its muscles

39

THE NORTH

From aye-ayes to gorillas: the Durrell Wildlife Conservation Trust

tacular smaller animals. Tours highlight the finite nature of the world's animal resources. One of the zoo's main goals is to breed endangered species and it runs an exchange and breeding programme with Melbourne zoo. *Daily 9.30am–5pm, April–Oct until 6pm | £16 | www.durrell.org*

LA MARE WINE ESTATE ★
(130 A2) (*D10*)

Made possible thanks to the climate brought in by the Gulf Stream, four wines of acceptable quality plus a sparkling variety and a cider bear the beautifully designed stickers of this small wine estate. The owners invite visitors to come and look behind the scenes. When you visit the shop, don't miss the chance to buy a jar of home-made black butter, a black spread made from cider, apples and spices – or the self-distilled liqueurs. If you come in the afternoon, be sure to order a slice of cake. *Mid-April–Oct daily 10am–5pm | free entry, guided tour through the winery and distillery with wine tasting £9 | www.lamarewineestate.com*

land of Madagascar. Here, in the twilight you can just see the dishevelled primate, which is active at night, and not loved in its native country because of its looks: it's a magical moment. Other types of lemur – active during the day – tumble around outside, and the gorillas are especially fascinating. The park-like grounds increase the slightly unreal, paradisiacal impression that this unusual zoo makes on its visitors. Concrete replicas of dodos – the flightless bird that was exterminated in the 17th century – serve as a memorial to all extinct species, and act as an emblem for the zoo's eccentric collection, which also extends to less spec-

FOOD & DRINK

LES FONTAINES (130 B1) (*E10*)
A large, rustic 15th-century pub that offers typical pub food in a relaxed, child-friendly atmosphere. *Daily | Route de Nord | St John | tel. 01534 86 27 07 | Budget–Moderate*

HUNGRY MAN ● (131 E2) (*J11*)
This regular-looking food stall in Rozel Bay serves every possible type of fast food – including vegetarian meals and gourmet burgers. The long line of people waiting outside testify to its popularity. Some islanders will come here just to enjoy a cream tea – it's the cheapest anywhere on Jersey. *Daily during the holiday season | Rozel Bay | Budget*

40

JERSEY

ST MARY'S COUNTRY INN
(130 A2) (*m* D11)
A cosy guesthouse serving tasty meals, including scallops wrapped in bacon. It's the best pub in the north of the island. Order a hoppy Liberation Ale and make a toast to Jersey's liberation from the German occupation. Live music on Fridays. *Daily | La Rue des Buttes | St John | tel. 01534 48 28 97 | Budget–Moderate*

SPORTS & ACTIVITIES

INSIDER TIP ▶ CIDER APPLE ORCHARD
(131 D2) (*m* G11)
This spot near Trinity Parish Church makes a fine place for a picnic. The National Trust planted 120 apple trees here in order to preserve the old variety of cider fruit. *La Rue du Mont Pellier*

DIVING (131 D2) (*m* G10)
The best underwater views in the deep, secluded bays of the north coast are had when a northeasterly wind is blowing. Hire diving gear and suits from the *Bouley Bay Dive Centre (tel. 01534 86 69 90 | www.scubadivingjersey.com)* in Bouley Bay. The centre also takes divers out in a boat.

BEACHES

BONNE NUIT BAY (130 C1) (*m* F10)
A small jewel of a bay with colourful boats, a sand and gravel beach, and a busy beach café *(all-day until 9pm | Budget–Moderate)* that serves crab rolls throughout the day. In the afternoon you can get tasty Thai cuisine (the owner is Thai).

BOULEY BAY
(131 D–E2) (*m* G–H 10–11)
A beautiful bathing bay with a predominantly stony beach. There's a hotel, a pub and a small diving school. There's always something going on until the afternoon at the *Mad Mary* kiosk – a typical island food stall that's run with passion – because the food is tasty and the ambience sociable.

GRÈVE DE LECQ (129 F1) (*m* C10)
A typical half-moon-shaped bay on the north shoreline, even with a sandy beach at low tide. Horse-riders gallop by the water; the fishermen haul their boats high up the beach at high tide. There's also a café, the *Prince of Wales Hotel (14 rooms | tel. 01534 48 22 78 | www.princeofwalesjersey.com | Moderate)*, a pub and an old defensive tower.

LOW BUDGET

A guided walking tour is an affordable highlight of any visit to the island. The themed guided tours are mainly about the fabulous flora and (ocean) fauna, adventure and food (see p. 112). *www.jersey.com/guided-walks-in-jersey*

Bikes *(from £14 per day | short.travel/kai14)* are better than rental cars on Jersey. They cost less, and everything on the island is set up for cyclists, with good cycle maps, marked routes and the right of way on country roads. The compact bus network is even cheaper *(from £2.20, day ticket £8 | www.libertybus.je)*.

The old mill in Grève de Lecq has long been a quaint pub and restaurant. On Sundays *(noon–3pm)*, the islanders can enjoy a Sunday roast here for a tenner! *Le Moulin de Lecq | tel. 01534 48 28 18*

THE NORTH

PLÉMONT BAY (129 D–E1) (*B9–10*)
At low tide, the steep north coast's westernmost bathing bay has a beautiful sandy beach that's great for kids. Steps lead down to the wide bay, with INSIDER TIP caves to explore below and a friendly café above serving tasty cakes and breakfasts. Even at high tide you can enjoy the superb view, and the coastal hiking path crossing the bay – a one-hour undulating route to Grève de Lecq – is spectacular.

ROZEL BAY (131 E2) (*J11*)
With its brightly painted houses and boats, this beautiful, small seaside community is reminiscent of a village on a Greek island. There's a dizzyingly deep harbour, the brilliantly kitschy *Hungry Man* kiosk, and the busy *Rozel Pub (closed Sun evening | tel. 01534 86 34 38 | www.rozelpubanddining.co.uk | Moderate)*, the restaurant there has one of the best cuisines in the north.

ENTERTAINMENT

After the hike, it's time to go to the pub – until the last bus departs. In the cosy *Rozel Pub* in Rozel the visitors mingle with locals. It's similar in the converted pub and restaurant, *Moulin de Lecq* in Grève de Lecq. The German army already used its 18-t mill stone to produce electricity. Nobody mentions this when you enjoy a toast with the locals!

WHERE TO STAY

CHÂTEAU LA CHAIRE (131 E2) (*H11*)
This oak-panelled hotel – perhaps the most romantic on the island – looks like a country house. The cellar contains Mouton Rothschild red wine, and there's a wild garden designed in 1841 by the botanist Samuel Curtis, director of London's Kew Gardens. Situated on Jersey's rugged northeast coast, the hotel has an air of exclusive elegance

Walk down the steps – at low tide! – to Plémont Bay on Jersey's north westernmost tip

JERSEY

and a certain Sleeping Beauty charm. 14 individually furnished rooms; some with private balconies. *Rozel Bay | tel. 01534 86 33 54 | www.chateau-la-chaire.co.uk | Expensive*

INSIDER TIP DURRELL WILDLIFE CAMP (131 D3) (*H11*)

Do you fancy camping in a zoo, in a roomy luxury tent? You'll feel like you're on safari if you stay the night in the yurts with their wood ovens near the lemur's lakeside habitat. Entry to the zoo is also included in the price, as are the guided tours that start at dawn and dusk. 3 nights from £480 (two adults and two children). *tel. 01534 86 00 90 | www.durrell.org*

INSIDER TIP LA CRÊTE FORT
(130 C1) (*F10*)

Live like an island Seigneur – snuggle up in the refreshing summer evening without WIFI: it was built in 1843 as a defence against the French. Until 2006, this was the residence of the royal vice-governor, and now the fort belongs to Jersey's heritage accommodation locations. Stay here as a couple or a group of five, you feel on top of the world high above the north shoreline and Bonne Nuit Bay. Functional, but not austere, with a banqueting hall, viewing platform, car park and kitchen. 3 nights from £600. *Tel. 01534 6 33 30 47 | www.jerseyheritage.org*

ROZEL CAMPING PARK
(131 E2) (*J11*)

Rent a permanently installed fixed tent with gas, refrigerator and more (*5 days | 2 pers. from £340*). The site includes a swimming pool, shops and playgrounds. Stay with your own tent from *£13. St Martin | tel. 01534 85 67 97 | www.rozelcamping.com*

UNDERCLIFF GUEST HOUSE
(131 D2) (*G11*)

This beautiful guesthouse is an ideal stop for hikers making their way along the north coast. Also self catering tourist accomodation available. *13 rooms | Bouley Bay | tel. 0800 1 12 30 58 | www.undercliffjersey.com | Moderate*

THE EAST

The morning sunshine lights up a coastline with its omnipresent flat beaches. The sea recedes at low tide to expose a mile-long sandy landscape that is overlooked by Martello towers.

Gorey, the only noteworthy village on the east coast, is the best place to watch the sun's daily spectacle. The castle, the harbour and wheeling gulls combine to form a dramaric setting. The east coast of the island is a place for gentle exploration. You can walk for several hours along the beach of the large Royal Bay of Grouville. Count the old defensive towers as you go, or perhaps keep a tally of the people walking their dogs in the tideland. The more northerly bay between Le Saut Geoffroi viewpoint and St Catherine's Breakwater is smaller and offers beautiful views from the coastal road. If you take a trip into the interior, you'll come across dolmen, Neolithic graves.

SIGHTSEEING

DOLMEN DE FALDOUËT
(131 F4) (*J12–13*)

These almost 6,000 year-old grave sites are hidden a short way behind Gorey castle. The monument's 15 m-/49.2 ft-long corridor and its dolmen structure bears witness to the ancient history of human settlement on Jersey.

43

THE EAST

MONT ORGUEIL CASTLE ★
(131 F4) (*K13*)

This 13th-century castle is the most majestic sight on the island. It was designed to deter French attackers in the Hundred Years' War, and isn't that easy to get to even today! The stone steps leading up from the harbour are the more onerous of the two possible routes, but the well looked after castle is worth the little bit of perspiration needed to scale them. It's astonishing that the castle is still in remarkably good condition – after the invention of gunpowder, the walls didn't cut the mustard. However, the castle has always found dedicated fans, including Sir Walter Raleigh, who campaigned to preserve the building when he was the island's Goveneur in 1600. The castle was the island's very own Alcatraz for political prisoners during the French Revolution of 1789. Today, exhibitions display archaeological finds and reproductions of a siege. Climb to the top to enjoy get what might be the best view on the island, overlooking the town and harbour. *Daily 10am–4pm, March–Oct until 6pm | £12.55*

ST CATHERINE'S BREAKWATER
(131 F3) (*K11*)

This 800 m-/2,625 ft-long harbour wall was built in the mid-19th century as the Victorians' answer to the French fortifications in Cherbourg. The project was also meant to include a fortified harbour with a second wall close to Archirondel beach, but the arrival of steam ships, which required a deeper harbour, put an end to these grandiose plans. The vast pier attracts ● anglers, bottlenose dolphin and sunset walkers alike. Ex-angler David Cowburn has set up a turbot farm in a former German bunker. At the ◉ *Jersey Turbot Farm (tel. 01534 86 88 36)*, you can take a look and chat with the entrepreneur, who feeds his 6,000 or so turbot with organic fish food (register beforehand). **INSIDER TIP** Self caterers can buy fish here, when they call a day in avance or visit for the open day on Sunday (9am–5pm).

VICTORIA TOWER
(131 F4) (*J12–13*)

This small Martello tower stands high over the coast a little to the north of Gorey Castle and offers a fantastic backdrop for a **INSIDER TIP** picnic with a panoramic view. The view sweeps across from Catherine's Breakwater to the castle. The Dolmen de Faldouët isn't far away: you can walk to it from the castle by hiking over Mont de la Guérande. *Rue des Marettes*

FOOD & DRINK

CRABSHACK (131 F4) (*J13*)
The catch of the day, beef burgers and mussels are served behind the castle. *Closed Sun evening, Oct–March also Mon | Route de la Côte | tel. 01534 84 02 18 | Moderate*

DRIFTWOOD CAFÉ (131 F3–4) (*J12*)
Vitamin boost: a beachside breakfast and lunch café with fresh salads and barbecue. Perfect for breakfast. *Daily | Route de la Côte | Archirondel Bay | tel. 01534 85 21 57 | Budget*

ENTWHISTLES FISH & CHIPS
(131 F4) (*J13*)

This takeaway in Gorey village has been a hit with the locals for 30 years. Get them to pack you up a large portion of freshly battered fish and chips, and then take it down to the sea. You can devour the delicious contents on one of the benches among the flower beds, with a view of the castle on the left. *Closed Sundays. | Main Road | www.entwhistles.com | Budget*

44

JERSEY

The picturesque town is down below, while Jersey's most attractive viewing point is above: Mont Orgueil Castle

FEAST (131 F4) (*J13*)
Feast's good international cuisine is popular with the islanders. In summer, you can sit out by the harbour below the castle and eat mussels and steak as you watch the comings and goings of the tide. There's an open fire in winter. Book ahead! *Closed Tue | Gorey Pier | tel. 01534 611118 | www.feast.je | Moderate*

CAFÉ POSTE (131 F5) (*J13*)
Local turbot, lobster, beef and halloumi from Cypress: the diverse menu is extremely popular with islanders who like eating very good, unpretentious food. The old train building exudes a cosy, intimate atmosphere, including a candlelit dinner. *Closed Mon/Tue | Rue de la Ville ès Renauds | tel. 01534 85 96 96 | www.cafeposte.co.uk | Moderate*

SUMA'S (131 F4) (*J13*)
This small, sweet, unpretentious seaside cottage serves exquisite cuisine and some 80 wines. It is the best lunch spot on the east side of the island. Make sure to book! *Closed Sun evening | Gorey Hill | tel. 01534 85 32 91 | sumasrestaurant.com | Moderate–Expensive*

LEISURE & SPORTS

GOLF (131 F5) (*J13*)
Royal Jersey Golf Club: 18 holes, par 70, only with proof of handicap. *Tel. 01534 85 44 16 | www.royaljersey.com*

WATERSPORTS (131 F4) (*J13*)
You can rent kayaks and wakeboards or book trips in a speedboat at the *Gorey Watersports Centre (tel. 07700 84 47 73). www.goreywatersports.co.uk*

BEACHES

ROYAL BAY OF GROUVILLE
(131 F4–6) (*J13–14*)
A large, wide, sweeping sandy bay that's great for swimming. There's parking and toilets at La Roque and Gorey.

45

THE SOUTH

ST CATHERINE'S BAY
(131 F3–4) (*M J12*)
Anne Port and Havre de Fer's secluded bays are the islanders' INSIDER TIP first choice if they want to have a picnic on the beach. Both have toilets.

WHERE TO STAY

BEAUSITE HOTEL (131 F5) (*M J13*)
A comfortable mid-range hotel in a beautiful location near the Royal Jersey Golf Club. Children are expressly welcome. *76 rooms | Grouville Bay | tel. 01534 85 75 77 | www.beausitejersey.com | Moderate*

INSIDER TIP BEUVELANDE CAMPING SITE (131 E4) (*M H12*)
The island's best equipped camping site. The site includes fixed tents, caravans, a pool, a restaurant and a shop. *La Rue de Beuvelande | St Martin | tel. 01534 85 35 75 | www.campingjersey.com*

OLD BANK HOUSE HOTEL
(131 F4) (*M J13*)
At the heart of the village of Gorey, only a few minutes from the harbour, remote from the castle and restaurants, the accommodation is simple, but pleasant. English breakfast; in March, April and October also continental breakfast is served. *12 rooms | Gorey Village | tel. 01534 85 42 85 | www.oldbankhousejersey.com | Budget–Moderate*

THE SOUTH

The south, the best part of Jersey for tourists, is lined with large sandy beaches between the cosmopolitan St Helier, St Aubin and St Brelade.

Due to the shallow angle of the seabed in this region, the island gains and loses around one third of its area in the south every day. This means that the distance to the sea changes massively. St Aubin's

Follow your nose: you can take that literally with Jersey lavender

JERSEY

bay stretches out between the dinky town of St Aubin and the almost city-like St Helier. There's a rush hour on the costal road twice a day, which can be avoided by using the cycle path at the promenade.

Sailing, water skiing and windsurfing are the main activities here. There are a few larger hotels in St Brelade's Bay, but if you walk along the sea wall with its guesthouses, cafés and shops and into Ouaisné Bay, you'll feel a bit like you're on a quaint Greek island in the Aegean Sea. The interior of this part of Jersey includes the idyllic valley of St Peter, Waterworks Valley, and the parish villages of St Peter and St Lawrence.

SIGHTSEEING

HAMPTONNE COUNTRY LIFE MUSEUM
(130 B3) (*E11*)

It's worth taking the trip from Millbrook – located halfway round St Aubin's Bay – through the tree-lined Waterworks Valley with its three small reservoirs down to this museum farm in the island's centre. Performers in costume give you a personal insight into life on a farm in the island interior – and no Disneyland! Everything is as it used to be: stables, a tower-like dovecote, gardens, Jersey cows, a fruit orchard and apple press that was used to produce farmhouse cider. This tradition is preserved on the third weekend in October: the cider festival. You are invited to try the INSIDER TIP fruity, farmhouse cider and sometimes you can take away a small bottle. The farm is also a member of the fabulous self-catering accommodation managed by Jersey Heritage *(www.jerseyheritage.org)*: you can stay in comfortable lodgings – and the cockerel gives you an early-morning call! *May Sat/Sun 10am–4pm, June–mid-Sept daily 10am–5pm | £8.95 | short.travel/kai1*

JERSEY LAVENDER ● (129 F4) (*C13*)

Light sandy ground (and a willingness to take risks) was key to the setting up of this English lavender farm in the early 1980s. Everything revolves around the flower's aroma and taste on this family farm. You can experience the distillation of lavender and other oils before purchasing all conceivable types of products in the shop – they make excellent Jersey souvenirs. Sparkling lavender wine and meals spiced with the flower are also on offer. A small landscape garden with exotic trees sits next to the flower fields. The lavender is harvested from June to August. *May–mid-Sept Tue–Sun 10am–5pm | £3.20, June–Aug £5.90 | Rue du Pont Marquet | St Brelade | www.jerseylavender.co.uk*

JERSEY WAR TUNNELS ●
(130 B4) (*E12*)

This tunnel complex to the east of the attractive St Peter's Valley was cut into the rock by forced labourers from eastern Europe at the orders of Hitler's motorway builder, Fritz Todt. This prize-winning museum successfully recreates the horror of the time, using original sound recordings. You can walk through the tunnels and find out about the fate of islanders' by using copies of their identification papers. There's also a shop and a café. *March–Oct daily 10am–6pm, Nov 10am–4pm | £13 | Les Charrières de Malory | St Lawrence | www.jerseywartunnels.com*

JERSEY'S LIVING LEGEND VILLAGE
(130 A3) (*D12*)

Real hype about Jersey's history *(£7.50)*, professionally staged. Including go-carting *(£10)*, adventure golf *(£6.50)* and a shopping village. *April–Oct daily 9am–5pm | Rue du Petit l'Aleval | St Peter | www.jerseyslivinglegend.co.je*

47

THE SOUTH

LE MOULIN DE QUETIVEL
(130 A4) (*D12*)

A trip through the enchanting St Peter's Valley leads down to this fully functioning 14th-century water mill. The exhibition next door provides vivid explanations about Jersey's technology and farming of old. *Mid-May–mid-Sept Sat 10am–4pm | £3*

NOIRMONT POINT
(130 A6) (*D15*)

The plateau of the Noirmont peninsula to the south of St Aubin offers magnificent views and footpaths down to two bays: Belcroute Bay and Ouaisné Bay. At the top, check out the view of the German bunkers and defensive positions that have been left here as a memorial. As you descend towards the sea, the view sweeps down to the small Portelet Bay which can be reached via some steps. On leaving the bunkers – where you can abseil down – it's recommended that you take the path to the bird-rich area of Portelet Common. Squeezed in between the plateau and Portelet Bay, the *Old Portelet Inn (daily | tel. 01534 74 18 99 | Budget)* will entice you in for glass of cider and a bowl of home-made soup.

ST AUBIN'S FORT
(130 A5) (*D13–14*)

If you stay next to the sea in St Aubin, you'll have this 16th-century fortified gem in front of you each morning. Wait for low tide and walk the 500 m/1,640 ft across the bay to visit it yourself – you'll gain a new perspective on the landscape.

ST BRELADE'S PARISH CHURCH AND FISHERMEN'S CHAPEL ★
(129 F5) (*C13–14*)

This is one of the magical spots on the island. The chapel and graveyard make a wonderful ensemble that sits like a peaceful granite refuge above the lively activity of the beach volleyball players and the tides in the Channel below. The unadorned granite of the small church sets off the colourful windows created by local artist, H. T. Bosdet. The small chapel's single-aisled structure was probably built before the church next door. The frescoes in the barrel vault date from the 13th or 14th century.

FOOD & DRINK

LA BELLE GOURMANDE
(130 A5) (*D13*)

It sounds French and also offers French cheese at the deli counter. So, buy your essentials for a hiking picnic – after you've enjoyed (from 9am) an avocado toast or *shakshuka*. *Closed Mon | Charing Cross | St Aubin | www.labellegourmande.com | Budget–Moderate*

THE BOAT HOUSE (130 A5) (*D13*)

The liveliest, most modern restaurant on the cosy harbour. Brasserie style below and narrow rows of tables above. Sea views and good seafood. *Daily | One North Quai | St Aubin's Harbour | tel. 01534 74 42 26 | Moderate*

MARK JORDAN AT THE BEACH
(130 B4) (*E13*)

In the middle of the enormous St Aubin's Bay, this casual and romantic beachside bistro boasts the best service and cuisine in Jersey's culinary landscape. The wine and meals aren't overpriced considering their quality. Mark loves Jersey and its produce, which is why around 90 per cent of his ingredients come from the island – and as much as possible is grown in an environmentally friendly way. The vegetarian range of Mediterranean dishes is also delicious. *Daily | La Route de la Haule | tel. 01534 78 01 80 | www.markjordanatthebeach.com | Moderate*

JERSEY

OLD COURTHOUSE INN
(130 A5) (*D13*)
St Aubin's most solid restaurant. Sit enthroned directly over the harbour on one of its many floors – you'll feel as if you're in the belly of a ship. A great mix of rustic and upscale service, ambience and (international) cuisine. *Daily | tel. 01534 74 64 33 | www.oldcourthousejersey.com | Moderate*

OLD SMUGGLER'S INN
(129 F5–6) (*C14*)
This inn is a long-standing island institution – parts of the wall date from the 13th century. Drink a beer around the fire or settle down in front of large portions of Portiuguese inspired barbecue under low beams. *Daily | Ouaisné Bay | tel. 01534 74 15 10 | www.oldsmugglersinn.com | Budget-Moderate*

OYSTER BOX (129 F5) (*C13*)
This popular spot on the beachside promenade brings the very best of local produce to its many tables: oysters, hand collected scallops and fish caught by one of the island's last remaining fishermen. There's a relaxed beach atmosphere. *Daily | La Route de la Baie | St Brelade | tel. 01534 74 33 11 | Budget*

BEACHES

BEAUPORT ✹ (129 E5) (*C14*)
The name of this bay – which means "beautiful harbour" – certainly keeps its promise. Romantics will prefer to stay up near the car park and enjoy the view, while any pirates among you may be tempted to take the long walk down to the beach for the chance to meet the local yachties who sail into the bay for lunch.

OUAISNÉ BAY (129 F5) (*C14*)
You can only walk from the sandy beach at Ouaisné Bay to St Brelade's Beach at low tide. The tides will cut off the two swimming beaches for six hours. But the ✹ link path over the cliff-tops is fabulous and offers a wonderfully Mediterranean-like view. The view from the heathland ✹ Portelet Common goes far into the distance. The hiking tour starts at the car park in the bay. The *Dartford warbler* twitters high above.

PORTELET BAY (130 A6) (*D14*)
An idyllic small bay with an island and tower, situated to the east of Ouaisné Bay at the foot of Noirmont Point. A very steep path leads down to the bay. You can walk to the tower at low tide. Romantic!

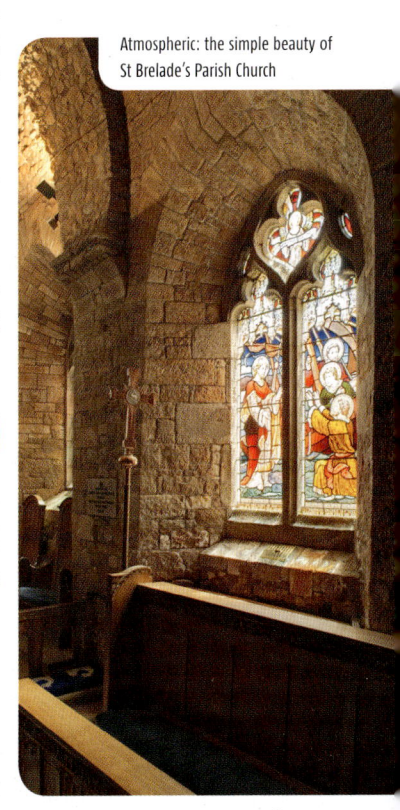

Atmospheric: the simple beauty of St Brelade's Parish Church

49

THE SOUTH

A small tower on a small island in a small bay: Portelet Bay

ST AUBIN'S BAY
(130 A–C 4–5) (*D–F13*)

At low tide, the widest beach on the island stretches out a good 5 km/3.1 mi between St Aubin and St Helier. The bay is Jersey's watersports hub, but you can also escape the busy coastal road and walk or cycle around to explore the little villages in the area.

ST BRELADE'S BAY (129 F5) (*C14*)

A magnificent beach for swimming in Jersey's most popular bay. The beach is on a gentle slope so the water heats up quickly. You can rent wind breaks, sun loungers and parasols.

ENTERTAINMENT

The nightlife in the small harbour of St Aubin is more down to earth than in St Helier. In the Tenby Bars pub, you'll even find a couple of quiet corners where you can flick through such books as Victor Hugo's Channel Island epic Toilers of the Sea. Half a dozen comfortable restaurants are strung together almost seamlessly. Enjoy an opulent dinner and then take a walk to watch the boats and fellow night owls strolling through town. In the low season, it's easy to get talking to the locals – and, who knows, perhaps you'll be invited to collect oysters with them at the weekend. You can party after sundown in the hotels around St Brelade's Bay.

WHERE TO STAY

INSIDER TIP BIARRITZ HOTEL
(129 F5) (*C13*)

This three-star Christian hotel (with no alcohol licence and prayer meetings every morning) is exceptionally popular thanks to its relaxed ambience, its good service, and its position high over the beach in St Brelade's Bay. The rooms are cosy but not too small. A staircase leads down to one of the most magnificent beaches on the island. There's a buffet on Sundays with a singing session afterwards (optional, of course!). *46 rooms | Le Mont Sohier |*

JERSEY

St Brelade's Bay | tel. 01534 74 22 39 | www.biarritzhotel.co.uk | Moderate

GOLDEN SANDS HOTEL
(129 F5) *(C13)*

It feels like a classic seaside hotel: directly above St Brelade's Bay with south-facing views and the sea ahead. It's best only to book one of these rooms – that's why you're here! The bay beneath your window becomes so wide at low tide that you think you could almost walk across to Saint Malo in France. The rooms are excellent with modern furnishings. Breakfast is delicious and the service is attentive. *62 rooms | La Route de la Baie | St Brelade | tel. 01534 74 12 41 | www.goldensandsjersey.com | Moderate–Expensive*

HARBOUR VIEW **(130 A5)** *(D13)*

A very cosy, small guesthouse right by the most beautiful harbour on the island. A 300-year-old house with 14 modern rooms and *Danny's*, a nice, small restaurant *(daily | Budget). Le Boulevard | St Aubin's Harbour | tel. 01534 74 15 85 | www.harbourviewjersey.com | Moderate*

SOMERVILLE HOTEL
(130 A5) *(D13)*

This hotel – with panoramic views of St Helier – stands like a white castle above St Aubin, Jersey's most colourful harbour. The restaurants are two minutes' walk away. There's a generous lounge, a pool, palm trees, a garden view at breakfast, and free bus transfers to St Brelade and St Helier. *59 rooms | Mont du Boulevard | St Aubin | tel. 01534 49 19 00 | www.dolanhotels.com | Moderate–Expensive*

WINDMILLS HOTEL **(129 F5)** *(C13)*

Situated high up in the steep, peaceful hinterland above St Brelade's Bay, a real magnet for visitors in the summer, the view from the balconies is magical; the rooms overlooking the garden also make you feel good. You also feel at home on the island. The bus stop is 200 m/656 ft away, and the big holiday-makers' bay is only ten minutes away on foot – but it's uphill on the way back ... *40 rooms | Mont Gras d'Eau | St Brelade | tel. 01534 74 42 02 | www.windmillshotel.com | Moderate*

ST HELIER

MAP INSIDE BACK COVER
(130 C5) *(F13–14)*

The capital city with a population of 28,000 is almost ostentatious with the modernised, glass harbour front.

With its magnificent location in a large sandy bay, St Helier has everything you could want from a seaside town. The fortified Elizabeth Castle, standing at the entrance to the harbour, bears witness to its strategic importance over the centuries. A road tunnel travels through the hill that juts out into the middle of the town. In 1966, a leisure centre was built within the walls of the old Fort Regent, which now looks like a UFO landed there. St Helier looks even more impressive when you get to the harbour. The strongly tidal sea is constantly being pushed back to expand the town or claim more land for mooring spots for the ever-growing number of yachts, as was the case when the new waterfront was built.

Not only is St Helier favoured by the Gulf Stream climate, but its once precarious status as the long-standing object of both English and French expansionist desires has turned to its cultural advantage: the islanders in St Helier have been coaxed out of their British reserve, something also aided by the money that flows into the town thanks to Jersey being a

ST HELIER

tax haven – a wealth attested to by the managers in their strict suits strutting along the island's streets.

SIGHTSEEING

BERESFORD FISH MARKET
(U C4) (*M c4*)
Although much smaller than the Central Market, this fish market's older halls and wonderful array of fish for sale make it an attractive destination. The variety of fresh seafood means there's always a fascinating – if sometimes bizarre – feast for the eyes. *Mon–Wed, Fri, Sat 7.30am–5.30pm, Thu 7.30am–2pm | Beresford Street*

CENTRAL MARKET (U C4) (*M c4*)
You can find sensibly used Victorian architecture in this beautiful market hall with its glass roof, Greek columns and iron supports. Apart from the typical market fare on offer, there's an excellent flower stall, where you can buy beautiful bouquets for your loved ones. *Mon–Wed, Fri, Sat 7.30am–5.30pm, Thu 7.30am–2pm | Halkett Place*

ELIZABETH CASTLE
(130 C5) (*M F14*)
This imposing fort lies half a mile from the harbour, on a rocky island in the sea. It was built at the end of the 16th century to replace the out-dated Gorey Castle and to protect against attacks on Jersey from the sea. During the English Civil War (1642–51), the Royalists – and the de Carteret family in particular – were forced to barricade themselves inside the castle to escape the Parliamentarians. A soldier's life was hard on the cliffs, but gradually improved over the centuries as the castle was modernised and connected to the water supply. A great many soldiers – in varying degrees of sobriety – drowned on their way between the town and the castle.

A secured causeway was built in the late 19th century. Visitors can use this

LIVING IN FORTS AND TOWERS

This varied range of historic buildings is a romantic option for self caterers: they're great for couples or groups of four to twelve people. There are currently more than a dozen enticing locations on Jersey, ranging from sparce sleeping bag hostels (Archirondel Tower, L'Etacquerel Fort for 30 hikers) to fully furnished apartments. The properties include: *Barge Aground* in St Ouen's Bay, a 1930s Art Deco villa for four persons in the shape of a boat; ● *Corbière Radio Tower*, a German occupation-era concrete radio transmission tower built in the Bauhaus style – ☼ the living room boasts a 360 degree view; the *Elizabeth Castle Apartment*, a castle on a small island off St Helier; *Fort Leicester*, a lonely coastal fort for eight persons in Bouley Bay. With basic amenities (no running water!), but in a dramatic setting in the sea are *Seymour Tower* (Royal Bay of Grouville) and *La Rocco Tower* (St Ouen's Bay) – a local guide across the sands is compulsory. The prices differ widely: from £63 in bunk beds on the sand to £1800 *(6 people/1 week)* at the Hamptonne Country Life Museum. *www.jerseyheritage.org/holiday*

JERSEY

750 m/2,461 ft breakwater at low tide or let themselves be transported over to the castle in puddle duck boats when the sea is in. The castle's highlight is the Hermitage chapel, which can be reached by a second causeway. The monk St Helier is said to have stayed here in the 6th century. *Mid-March–Oct daily 10am–5.30pm | £11.60, £14.35 with the ferry | www.jerseyheritage.org*

JERSEY MUSEUM & ART GALLERY
(U B4) (*b4*)

The three floors of this outstanding modern museum illustrate the richness of Jersey's history. Includes exhibits of art, history, social history, and the bizarre. You can also hear the old island dialect of Jérrais. *Core hours daily 10am–4pm | £9.95| The Weighbridge | www.jerseyheritage.org*

MARITIME MUSEUM ★
(U B5) (*b5*)

If you only visit one museum in St Helier, then make sure it's this one! Its exhibits on everything to do with the ocean, boats, sailing and fishing are presented partly

Elizabeth Castle: St Helier's imposing outpost lies on a rocky island

in a light-hearted, humorous way, and partly a scientific way – it's particularly fun for the kids! The *Occupation Tapestry Gallery* is housed in the same building. In the same spirit as the famous Bayeux Tapestry in Normandy, twelve new, hand-woven tapestries represent the twelve island parishes at the time of the German occupation. The artists, who sewed in teams, worked from photographs in such an accurate way that some occupation survivors have recognized themselves in the artworks. *Mid-March–Oct daily 10am–5pm, Nov–mid-March Sun 10am–4pm | £9.95 | New North Quay | www.jerseyheritage.org*

ST HELIER

FOOD & DRINK

BOHEMIA (U C5) (*c5*)
The hottest tip for gourmets in St Helier – the Bohemia is one of the three Michelin

Pullovers, pralines, pearl jewellery: Jersey's mini shopping metropolis St Helier

star restaurants of the island. If you want to watch Steve Smith's cooking at close quarters, book the Chef's table in the kitchen. The restaurant belongs to The Club Hotel & Spa. *Daily | Green Street | tel. 01534 87 65 00 | www.bohemiajersey.com | Expensive*

GREEN OLIVE (U A–B4) (*a–b4*)
A small, excellent restaurant with focus on vegetarian dishes. Also offers fusion cuisine and reasonably priced wines. *Closed Sun/Mon and Sat Midday | 1 Anley Street | tel. 01534 72 81 98 | www.greenoliverestaurant.co.uk | Budget–Moderate*

LONGUEVILLE MANOR ★ ● ◉
(131 D5) (*G13–14*)
Before you eat, whet your appetite with a walk through this 14th-century manor house's enormous vegetable garden! It will make the taste buds tingle. The garden provides many of the delicacies served in the wonderful country house kitchen, which has a lovely romantic ambience. Chef Andrew Baird prioritises eco-friendly farming and contact with local producers over everything else. *Daily | Longueville Road | St Saviour | tel. 01534 72 55 01 | www.longuevillemanor.com | Expensive*

ROSEVILLE BISTRO (U C6) (*c6*)
Simple and popular – this is hard to beat for its affordable fish meals. The bistro is located right by the water and opens from 6pm until midnight. *Daily | 86 Roseville Street | tel. 01534 87 42 59 | Budget–Moderate*

INSIDER TIP RUBY'S (U B4) (*b4*)
Broadway goes Jersey: the waiters and waitresses here can sing and act, as the boss Tonika Lawrence is a British film star. The rooms, atmosphere and cocktails are more Great Gatsby or Cabaret than trendy or millennial. The kitchen only serves fresh and, if possible, regional food. *Closed Sun/Mon | 57 New Street | tel. 01534 62 57 75 | Moderate*

INSIDER TIP THAI DICQ SHACK
(131 D5) (*G14*)
Jersey's hottest sunset spot! Some islanders swear that this is the best food to be had anywhere on Jersey. It's a simple kiosk right by the sea – the spiciest Asian

JERSEY

picnic in the Channel Islands! Make sure to get a bottle of wine from the supermarket first. *Daily | Dicq Slipway | tel. 01534 73 02 73 | Budget*

SHOPPING

KING STREET (U B4) (*m b4*)
Although all the facades on King Street look old and quaint, you'll feel the rush of big city shopping when you pass by the often exquisite window displays. You can buy anything here. There are shoes like sculptures, myriad perfumes, whole shops full of soap, dangerously enticing jewellery displays and the creations of international fashion designers. You'll almost forget you're on a small island and not in a booming shopping metropolis.

LIBERTY WHARF (U B4) (*m b4*)
Jersey's only covered mall lies in a central location between the harbour and the bus station. It was built at a cost of £350 million on a site that was dredged up from the harbour. It brings a touch of big city shopping to the town of St Helier. Cafés, a branch of Marks & Spencer, boutiques and the modern *Quayside Bistro* (*Moderate*) are all housed in this successful combination of classic and modern architectural styles.

LEISURE & SPORTS

AYUSH WELLNESS SPA ●
(U C2) (*m c2*)
Enjoy Ayurvedic meditation and treatments at the Hotel de France's beautiful spa. Hot stones, head massages, facial care, and a Gentleman's Energy Boost: this spa offers a whole range of Indian treatments. *From £84 | St Saviour's Road | tel. 01534 61 41 71 | www.defrance.co.uk/spa*

MUDFLAT HIKING ●
Thanks to the particularly strong tidal cycle that draws the sea a considerable distance from the shore, the mudflats of the east coast are a great place to explore when the tide is out. Head for the old defensive fortifications of *Icho* and *Seymour Tower*, which lie around 2 km/1.2 mi out in the Royal Bay of Grouville. The three-hour guided walking tours offer sweeping views of the coast. The insight you gain into the flora and fauna of Jersey's protected Ramsar sites is more interesting still. *May–Dec 3 to 4 times/month, also at night | from £16 | tel. 07797 85 30 33 | www.jerseywalkadventures.co.uk*

BEACH

GREEN ISLAND (131 D6) (*m G15*)
At high tide, Jersey's southernmost sandy beach is an absolute jewel of a place for swimming – it's particularly prized by the locals. Take the bus (line 1) or cycle the 3.5 km/2.2 mi on the coastal road to the southeast until you see a small signpost pointing to the car park. Afterwards, take refreshment in the *Green Island Restaurant (daily | tel. 01534 85 77 87 | greenisland.je | Moderate)*.

ENTERTAINMENT

You should at least pack a good shirt if you want to sample St Helier's nightlife – a collar is often required in the town's night clubs on Fridays and Saturdays. Clubs are usually open between 10pm and 2.30am. Before you go dancing, get into the swing of things in one of the town's numerous pubs – *Bellini's Jazz Bar* in Broad Street (live jazz until 11pm), for example. Live music can be heard in many bars in St Helier, at least at the weekend. The back room at *Chambers* in

ST HELIER

The drinks are in: nobody goes thirsty in St Helier's pubs

Mulcaster Street, for example, combines a pub atmosphere with a live band every evening. If you want to experience the trend for expensively furnished pubs and bars, check out *Tanguy's* on the same street, where hot DJs from England and the continent lay operate. For a more loungy and feminine atmosphere head for *Mimosa Bar* at the Liberty Wharf Centre. Here, the party starts with cocktails on Wednesdays. It's even worth just taking a walk around to check out the modern harbour quarter – new places are constantly opening.

WHERE TO STAY

HAMPSHIRE HOTEL (U C2) (📖 c2)
A good, mid-range hotel with a heated pool. Renovated in a modern colonial style. A few minutes' walk from the centre. *42 rooms | 53 Val Plaisant | tel. 01534 72 4115 | www.hampshirehotel.je | Moderate*

THE INN JERSEY (U B2) (📖 b2)
This boutique hotel, which has won awards for its high quality and its reliably good service, offers a good restaurant, sufficient parking and nice and modern rooms for a relatively low price, if booked online. Free tapas are served to accompany the live music on Fridays. *36 rooms | Queens Road | tel. 01534 72 22 39 | www.theinnjersey.com | Moderate*

OMMAROO HOTEL (U C6) (📖 c6)
The Victorian façade with palm-like cabbage palm trees is on the coast road; the beach and tidal pool Havre des Pas are

JERSEY

only across the road, Portuguese food is only 100 m/328 ft away at Moita's and the Thai Dicq Shack. *86 rooms | Havre des Pas | tel. 01534 72 34 93 | www.ommaroo.com | Moderate*

INFORMATION

VISIT JERSEY (U B4) (*b4*)
Liberation Bus Station | Esplanade | tel. 01534 85 90 00 | www.jersey.com

WHERE TO GO

ERIC YOUNG ORCHID FOUNDATION (131 D3) (*G12*)
The orchids grown by the late collector and scientist Eric Young blossom in a large greenhouse. Follow the signs from the A 8. *Wed–Sat 10am–4pm | £4.80 | www.ericyoungorchid.org*

LA HOUGUE BIE ★ (131 E4) (*H13*)
Make sure to duck your head when you enter the oldest remaining structure on the island, a corridor grave that was built sometime around 3000 BC *(mid-March–Oct daily 10am–5pm | £8.25 | www.jerseyheritage.org)*. You should also take the plunge and go inside the 15 m-/49.2 ft-high hill that towers over the grounds. The megalithic grave consists of around 70 stones that enclose a 10 m-/32.8 ft-long corridor and a large chamber.

The affiliated museum tells you more about the INSIDER TIP find of Celtic coins (50 BC) from 2012 with 70,000 pieces taken altogether. A monument to the victims of Nazi slave labour has been erected inside a former German bunker. *www.jerseyheritage.org*

SAMARÈS MANOR AND GARDENS (127 D5–6) (*G14*)
A must for gardeners and herbalists, this is also a popular destination for families because of it nature quiz, willow labyrinth and working animals. Apart from the herb garden, the manor house also has a Japanese garden and a water garden, and turns Jersey's famous long Jack cabbage – a plant as tall as a man – into INSIDER TIP traditional walking sticks. You can also take a tour through the house. *April–mid-Oct daily 9.30am–5pm | £9.75, with tour of the Manor House £13.70 | www.samaresmanor.com*

DAILY COASTAL PICNIC

Along the coastline that stretches for 75 km/46.6 mi you find plenty of spots to enjoy the views and picnic. You can pack ingredients from breakfast or buy provisions *en route* and store them in the bicycle basket or rucksack. The old coastal towers along the Royal Bay of Grouville often have snack bars. At Fliquet Bay in the far north-east there is the long St Catherine's Breakwater or Cape La Coupe Point. At L'Étacq in the north-west Faulkner Fisheries serves oysters natural (£1) and grilled (£1.50) throughout the day. On the cliffs between the sandy bays Ouaisné Bay and St Brelade's Bay you can find 🌿 viewing bench. The high areas on 🌿 Portelet Common and 🌿 Noirmont Point either side of Portelet Bay offer panoramic views during your picnic. Fish is delicious from the Cabin Café, about 1 km/0.6 mi east of St Aubin, and directly on the beach.

57

GUERNSEY

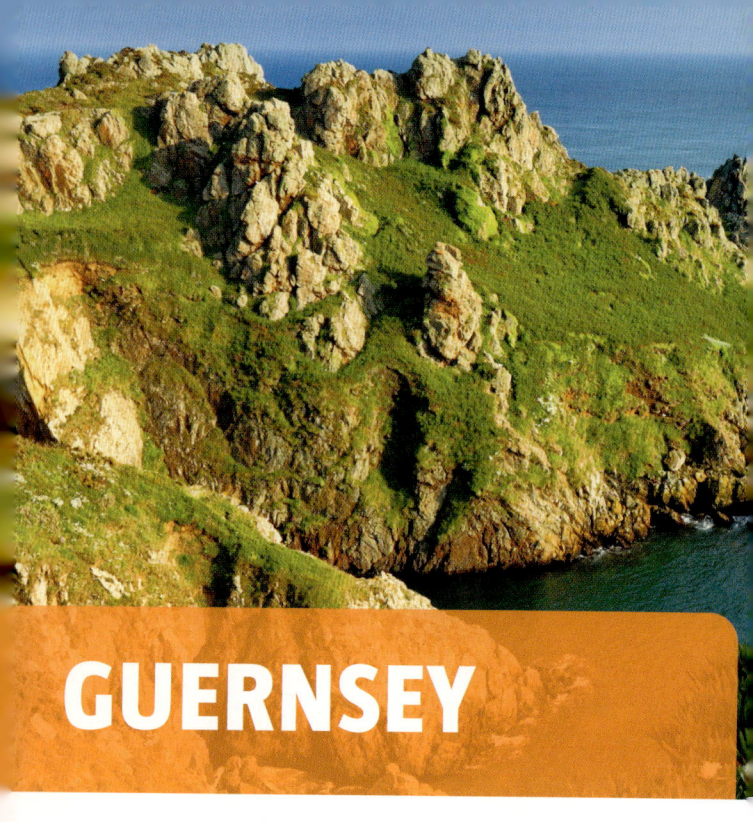

When the sky's crystal clear and the clouds look freshly laundered, you can look out from Guernsey over to Normandy, around 45 km/28 mi away.

Measuring in at 25 mi^2, Guernsey is the second largest Channel Island. Its proximity to France and its affiliation with the British Crown give it an elegant charm and unique political status. It feels a tad more French than Jersey – even when you compare the capitals of St Peter Port and St Helier. Guernsey's landscape is more gentle and detailed than Jersey's, with cyclists having the right of way on the labyrinth of *ruettes tranquilles* that criss-cross the island's interior.

Like Jersey, Guernsey is also a Bailiwick, a Royal Protectorate independent of both Great Britain and the EU. Herm, Sark and Alderney also belong to Guernsey in varying political categories. They are well worth visiting on day excursions by ferry or plane (Alderney). Guernsey and its three small satellites had a magnetic effect on the wealthy British after the end of the Second World War and the German occupation. Famous celebrities purchased hidden estates – it was chic to buy in the *Channel*. However, meanwhile the market, created especially for seriously wealthy island lovers, is saturated.

Most of the ordinary 65,000 Guernsey islanders are relatively prosperous and unemployment is low. Thanks to its financial operations, Guernsey has blossomed into a prosperous island. 60 per cent of its economic wealth comes from banking and IT,

Savoir-vivre and British eccentricity: fine, sandy beaches, dramatic cliffs and cottages straight from the set of an Agatha Christie film

14 per cent comes from tourism, and just seven per cent is earned through flower sales and farming – both former flagship trades on the island. Abandoned, overgrown greenhouses often serve as signs of agricultural decline.

Like on Jersey, however, the shameless boom years of managing tax-free millions are over. But Guernsey, unlike Jersey, still doesn't levy value added tax to balance the financial trading deficits.

Guernsey is split into ten parishes. It's an island of two faces: the south coast is characterised by its steep cliffs and picturesque cliff-top paths, while the northwest coast is reminiscent of Long Island with its wide beaches, soft light, waving marram grass, and pink-hued rocks.

Just as soon as the second-largest tidal cycle in the world retreats for the day, oyster catchers and curlews come out to stalk their prey through the sand on their thin legs, cormorants dry their wings on the cliffs. Many migratory birds spend the winter in this mild climate, which boasts around 2,025 hours of sun each

THE SOUTH

year. They fly off in spring when the first daffodils and bluebells bloom and the holiday season begins.

About 300,000 holidaymakers will find an island not overrun with tourists. The bays in the south are still as picturesque as in 1883 when Auguste Renoir painted bathers in Moulin Huet.

at the side of the road. The latter contain fresh vegetables, cut flowers and seasonal fruit – you just leave some money and help yourself.

The south, "Guernsey's garden", is separated into four parishes: St Andrew (pop. 2,400), the only parish without coastal access; Torteval (pop. 1,000)

A strange mosaic of shells, broken glass and porcelain: Little Chapel

Somehow, on Guernsey even time seems to have plenty of time. Since the settlements on Guernsey have no distinct local characteristics, this chapter travels clockwise through the points on the compass – taking its start and end point at St Peter Port, Guernsey's only town.

THE SOUTH

In Guernsey's agricultural south you'll find granite farmyards, greenhouses with ripening grapes and honesty boxes

the smallest parish with a Scottish-looking plateau; Forest (pop. 1,500); and St Martin (pop. 6,300). The most heavily populated, St Martin, is not just the most prosperous, but also the most beautiful parish with its stately homes, classic cars, and the kind of traditional stone cottages that Miss Marple would be proud to call home.

The south is a region for romantics and hikers alike. Gorse-lined pathways lead along the coast, lonely bays attract would-be Robinson Crusoes, and hotels serve elegant cream teas. Forest is a dra-

GUERNSEY

matic region where steep cliffs plunge down into the sea. The area takes its name from the forested regions that were once common in the parish, but few of these stand today.

SIGHTSEEING

GERMAN MILITARY UNDERGROUND HOSPITAL (127 D5) (*m* E6)
The hammering was heard deep into the night: forced labourers had to dig 2 km/1.2 mi of tunnels through earth and rock over 3 years. This eerie backdrop later housed a hospital for wounded German soldiers. A private museum with a great deal of atmosphere. *May–Oct daily 10am–4pm | £4 | www.germanundergroundhospital.co.uk*

GERMAN OCCUPATION MUSEUM (126 C5) (*m* D6)
Old signs, roll calls, guard rooms, uniforms, and wind-up telephones – this private museum near the church in Forest displays fascinating items from the German occupation. *Daily 10am–1pm, April–Oct until 4.30pm | £6 | www.germanoccupationmuseum.co.uk*

LA GRANDMÈRE DU CHIMQUIÈRE (127 E5) (*m* E6)
This 4,000 year-old menhir dates from a time when a belief in witches and ghosts was still very much alive. Requests for domestic happiness and fertility are still brought to the "grandmother of the graveyard" even today. She stands at the graveyard gate of St Martin's Parish Church.

LITTLE CHAPEL ● (126 C5) (*m* D6)
Measuring in at a length of just 5 m/16.4 ft, the Little Chapel in Les Vauxbelets is the smallest chapel in the world. It was started in 1914 by Déodat, a Catholic monk, and was intricately decorated with seashells and shards of glass and porcelain. It was completed about ten years later. *Visit for free at any time*

MARCO POLO HIGHLIGHTS

★ **Moulin Huet Bay**
A bay immortalised: Renoir painted it with passion → p. 63

★ **Sausmarez Manor**
Over 100 sculptures grace this Garden of Eden → p. 62

★ **Cliff paths**
45 km/28 mi of dreamy walkways between heaven and earth, gorse and sea → p. 63

★ **Cobo Bay**
The curtains rise for nature's very own show: splendid sunsets at Cobo Bay → p. 68

★ **Dolmen Le Déhus**
The product of sorcery, a place of ritual, or a devilish hangout? → p. 69

★ **St Peter Port**
A quaint combination of England and France → p. 72

★ **Castle Cornet**
The traditional cannon shot is fired here every day at noon → p. 74

★ **Hauteville House**
Haunted, dreamy, whimsical: the great Victor Hugo's white villa → p. 75

THE SOUTH

SAUSMAREZ MANOR ★
(127 E5) (*F6*)

Peter de Sausmarez is the current lord of this granite manor estate with its parkland in St Martin. His family has lived on the island ever since 1220. The manor house (£7) is home to different exhibitions: a collection of Victorian dolls houses, a railway for children, and – the highlight – the Park (£6), an outdoor collection of over 100 sculptures in glass, bronze, metal and granite that winds its way through the exotic looking garden. It's particularly worth a visit on Saturday mornings in summer: that's when there's a **INSIDER TIP** *market* selling all kinds of local produce. The excellent varieties of cheese and organic meat from 🌱 *Meadow Courts Farm* – a proponent of the slow food movement – are worth seeking out. And the manor house is also haunted (of course!): some evenings, the Seigneur himself leads a ghost tour through his eccentric home. *Gardens daily 10am–5pm, House April/May Mon–Thu 10.30am and 11.30am, June–Sept 10.30am, 11.30am and 2.30pm | £7.50 | www.sausmarezmanor.co.uk*

FOOD & DRINK

THE AUBERGE 🌱 (127 E5) (*F6*)

Start off at Jerbourg Point and take some time to enjoy the sunset as well as the 270-degree view of Moulin Huet Bay and the coastline as it meanders on to St Peter Port. Then take an aperitif on the lawn of this thoroughly relaxed top restaurant before going inside to enjoy dinner with a view of the lights of St Peter Port and Castle Cornet. The cuisine is French, and all the ingredients come straight from the sea or from Guernsey's market gardens. A two-course lunch costs just £16.95. *Daily | Jerbourg Road | St Martin | tel. 01481 23 84 85 | www.theauberge.gg | Moderate*

Venerable ancestral views: to the manner born in Sausmarez Manor

GUERNSEY

FERMAIN BEACH CAFÉ (127 E5) (*M F6*)
Relaxed beach café at the end of a slip road heading towards the coast. The food here matches the magnificence of the bayside location. Everything from the appetisers to the fish and the ice cream tastes so good that it's worth the walk – about an hour from St Peter Port on the coastal path or a short hop from the car park. It's also a great **INSIDER TIP stopover for a cocktail** (Hugo Spritz £7). *March–Oct daily 10am–6pm | Fermain Bay | tel. 01481 23 86 36 | Budget*

THE FARMHOUSE (126 C5) (*M D6*)
This former farm in the island's southern centre has been turned into a large restaurant and an exquisite small country hotel *(14 rooms | Moderate)*. They serve cuisine from the land (excellent pork) and the sea (try the turbot). Live jazz and weddings at the weekend; dinner served by the pool. *Daily | Route des Bas Courtils | St Saviour | tel. 01481 26 41 81 | www.thefarmhouse.gg | Moderate*

SHOPPING

CATHERINE BEST (127 E4) (*M F5*)
This goldsmith has collected numerous prizes for her jewellery. She also makes affordable pieces, including silver earrings from £53. *Steam Mill Lane | St Martin | www.catherinebest.com*

LEISURE & SPORTS

ICART POINT AND SAINTS BAY
(127 D–E6) (*M E7*)
A hiking destination with a view: the ☀ cliff-top path that winds its way down into Saints Bay starts opposite the Saints Bay Hotel. You can go over the cliffs in the opposite direction to ☀ Icart Point with its great sea views. Reward your efforts with high tea in Icart tea room.

CLIFF PATHS ★ ☀
Guernsey has a network of cliff-top paths that's almost almost 48 km/30 mi long. They were established in 1927, and an eight-man team takes care of their maintenance. One visit to the islands isn't enough to explore them all. The most beautiful time to walk is in the spring when wild flowers blossom on the cliffs and the bright sunlight allows you to enjoy distant views over the bays and the sea.

MOULIN HUET BAY ★ ●
(127 E5–6) (*M F6–7*)
Auguste Renoir painted the almost Mediterranean bay in 1883. Treat yourself to an impressionist afternoon: first, enjoy coffee in the luxurious garden of the Hotel Bella Luce, then walk for 1.5 km/0.9 mi to the bay through steep woodland where you will find a simple café amongst the hydrangea. On the hike back, not far from the Bella Luce, this time head for the excellent pub restaurant, The Captains, to learn some tips from the friendly locals.

PETIT BÔT BAY
(127 D5–6) (*M D–E 6–7*)
You reach the bay after a typical Guernsey walk: head to the airport by bus and then a few minutes' walk to the German Occupation Museum. Later, follow the road south-east and after ten minutes you will reach a group of cottages, magnolias, roses and camellias: the hamlet of Le Variouf. This area was rife with suspicion and full of witches. Canopies on house walls were places to crouch to win favour with the witches.
First, walk back a little to reach Petit Bôt Bay in 15 minutes via the Rue des Croise. The renovated coastal tower has an informative display about the tower's history and the almost shell-shaped bay has a sandy beach at low tide.

THE SOUTH

BEACHES

In the south and southwest of Guernsey, you'll find longer footpaths and sheltered, jewel-like beaches below the coastal cliffs. A cliff-top path connects the beaches of Fermain Bay with those at Moulin Huet Bay and Portelet Bay. Low tide reveals plenty of fine sand.

FERMAIN BAY (127 E5) (*M F6*)
This small beach lies 3 km/1.9 mi south of St Peter Port along a cliff path. Victor Hugo swam here. The bay is surrounded by woodland and has a small Martello tower.

PORTELET BAY (127 D6) (*M E7*)
This sheltered bay, about 2 km/1.2 mi across, has some wonderful small beaches. The path runs over fields and cliffs on its way from Icart Point to Pointe de la Moye.

SAINTS BAY (127 D–E6) (*M E–F7*)
From the Saints Bay car park, walk down to Saints Bay's white beach – a secluded swimming spot.

ENTERTAINMENT

FERMAIN TAVERN (127 E5) (*M F6*)
This large pub has presented the best live music on Guernsey already since the 1980s: Even Sir Elton John has made an appearance here, packing the lounge bar to the rafters. It's well worth a visit, even if it's just to enjoy a quiet drink in the pub's other bar. *Fort Road | www.fermaintavern.com*

WHERE TO STAY

LA BARBARIE HOTEL (127 D5) (*M E6*)
A romantic, stone-built hotel with prize-winning cuisine and 23 comfortable rooms. *Saints Road | St Martin | tel. 01481 23 52 17 | www.labarbariehotel.com | Expensive*

HOTEL BELLA LUCE (127 D5) (*M E6*)
A romantic old, four-star country hotel set in a magnificent garden with a swimming pool. In contrast to its olde-worlde exterior, the interior is decorated in a modern Scandinavian style. *31 rooms | La Fosse | St Martin | tel. 01481 23 87 64 | www.bellalucehotel.com | Expensive*

INSIDER TIP THE CAPTAIN'S (127 D5) (*M E6*)
A charming, old style country guesthouse with modern, individually tailored rooms

---

LOW BUDGET

Numerous restaurants offer reasonably priced "early bird" meals between 5pm and 7pm in St Peter Port: two-course menus (sometimes with a glass of wine) cost £10–18.

As elsewhere, the cheapest way to stay on Guernsey is in a tent (from around £13/person). Two beautiful campsites in natural surroundings are: *Fauxquets Farm (tel. 01481 25 54 60 | www.fauxquets.co.uk)* between St Andrew and St Saviour and *La Bailloterie Camping (tel. 01481 24 36 36 | www.campinginguernsey.com)* in St Sampson, which throws parties in the summer with boules and live music.

The public buses offer unrivalled value for money: a single journey costs £1, no matter how far you go, a day ticket costs £4.50. *www.buses.gg*

GUERNSEY

in the middle of sweet St Martin. Before the excellent dinner (delicious mackerel!) socialise with the locals who drink their beer here after work and are happy to give you the odd tip. *9 rooms | La Fosse de Haut | St Martin | tel. 01481 23 89 90 | www.thecaptainshotel.co.uk | Budget*

LE CHÊNE HOTEL
(126–127 C–D5) *(ɯ D6)*

A simple, friendly country hotel with a pool and restaurant near the airport and the woods. Great local atmosphere. From three nights the scooters, bikes and fishing rods are available for free. Also for self-catering guests. *26 rooms | Forest Road | Forest | tel. 01481 23 55 66 | www.lechene.co.uk | Budget–Moderate*

SAINTS BAY HOTEL (127 D6) *(ɯ E7)*

It's no mirage: this hotel really is in a breathtaking location above Saints Bay. The cliff paths begin right in front. *36 rooms | Icart Point | St Martin | tel. 01481 23 88 88 | www.saintsbayhotel.com | Moderate*

THE WEST

With its long beaches, soft winds and large picture windows, Guernsey's west coast is a quintessential holiday destination.

Nature stages an unforgettable show each day when the sun sinks over the horizon – every balcony becomes a front-row seat. This part of the island is made up of three parishes. First is the large, sea-orientated Castel (pop. 9,000) with long beaches and Cobo Bay – perfect for swimming in summer. Then comes St Saviour (pop. 2,700), ideal for fishing with its rocky bays, boats and small captains' houses. And, finally, St-Peter-in-the-Wood (St-Pierre-du-Bois, pop. 2,200)

Romantic residence with a wonderful garden: Hotel Bella Luce

with its profitable oyster bank in Portelet Harbour.
Unfortunately, cycling along the coastline is restricted due to the very narrow coastal road. Across the centre of the island, in about half an hour, you arrive in Cobo Bay from St Peter Port.

SIGHTSEEING

DOLMEN LE TRÉPIED (126 B4) *(ɯ B5)*
This 6 m-/19.7 ft-long corridor grave from the 3rd century BC sits in Perelle Bay. The capstones and supporting stones still stand today.

FORT GREY SHIPWRECK MUSEUM
(126 A5) *(ɯ B6)*
The waters around the islands are dangerous and claim lives even today. This museum in Fort Grey tower – built in 1803 – vividly represents the history of

65

THE WEST

the shipwrecks off Guernsey's coast. *April–Oct daily 10am–4.30pm | £4*

INSIDER TIP ▶ LIHOU ISLAND
(126 A3–4) (*m A4–5*)
Cut off from the west coast by the tide and home to the ruins of a monastery, this island is a protected Ramsar wetland. You can spend the night here in Youth Hostel-style accommodation. The two-hour round walk from the car park of the Fort Saumarez to Lihou is highly recommended. You'll learn a lot about the history, fauna and flora of this part of the coast. Gill Girard leads tours in summer *(www.gillgirardtourguide.com)* – find out more information at the Tourist Office. Hikers must keep an eye on the tide charts. *www.lihouisland.com*

PLEINMONT PLATEAU
(126 A5) (*m A–B6*)
Reminiscent of the west coast of Scotland, this plateau has dramatic views, a network of hiking routes, and is crossed by the offshoots of various coast paths. The ● *Pleinmont Tower (April–Oct Sun 2pm–5pm | £3.50)*, high above the plateau, houses an exhibition about the Atlantic Wall – a system of German coastal defences during Second World War. Built in 1942, the round, concrete tower, with numerous observation slits, has been kept in fine fettle by the Occupation Society since the war. The society's chairman, Richard Heaume, sometimes sells tickets to the tower. He played in the German bunker complex as a child and collected pistols, uniform jackets and officers' stripes – a hoard he later expanded with mortars, launchers and vehicles. His collection forms the basis of the German Occupation Museum in Forest. In the tower, you'll find telephones, binoculars, and examples of German propaganda, such as "Feind hört mit" (the enemy is listening). Items have been refurbished using original templates. Today, Guernsey's most imposing Nazi tower and defensive positions seem incongruous – an INSIDER TIP ▶ alien structure in a mix of Art Deco and Bauhaus styles.

INSIDER TIP ▶ SAUMAREZ PARK
(127 D3) (*m E4*)
Although Guernsey's largest park has a manor house at its heart, it is publicly owned. The former owner, a British ambassador to Japan, planted the park's giant camellias and magnolias. A piece of old Guernsey lives on in the Folk and Costume Museum. There's a path leading down into Cobo Bay. *Free entry to the Park, Museum mid-March–Oct daily 10am–5pm | £6 | www.nationaltrust.gg/places-to-visit*

BEAUTIFUL BILLS

Although the invisible credit of financial institutions is the Channel Islands' lifeblood, their bank notes are real head turners. Jersey created a new range of bank notes in different pastel tones in 2010. A Jersey cow has been included as the watermark. The bills are valued at 1, 5, 10, 20 and £50, and show a portrait of the Queen and a few historical landmarks. The notes of the States of Guernsey also show the Queen and different building motifs. Island notes aren't readily accepted on the mainland, and the coins aren't accepted at all.

GUERNSEY

The shipwreck museum in Fort Grey proves how treacherous the waters of the English Channel are

ST APOLLINE'S CHAPEL
(126 B4) (*C5*)
The renovated little chapel, a beautiful fresco from the pre-Reformation period is consecrated to the martyr Apollonia, the patron saint of dentists. *Free access during the day*

FOOD & DRINK

COBO FISH 'N' CHIPS (126 C3) (*D4*)
Locals love to buy the fish and chips from this shop right on the beach in Cobo Bay. *Daily*

LA RÉUNION (126 C3) (*D4*)
Together with Rockmount pub, this is *the* hotspot of the west coast. There is a fabulous view over Cobo Bay. The monkfish, turbot and Herm oysters couldn't be fresher. If you've had enough of seafood, enjoy the lamb and beef steak with Jersey potatoes. *Daily | Cobo Coast Road | Castel | tel. 01481 25 56 00 | Moderate*

SHOPPING

INSIDER TIP ▶ LE TRICOTEUR
(126 A5) (*B6*)
Treat yourself to a real Guernsey pullover (£80), the garment Admiral Nelson once ordered his sailors to wear. Elizabeth I wore Guernsey knitwear at the execution of Mary Queen of Scots, who was also wearing Guernsey stockings on her way to the gallows. *Copper Craft Centre | Rocquaine Bay*

LEISURE & SPORTS

BIRD WATCHING
Bird-watching tours are organised by the Royal Society for the Protection of Birds. *www.rspbguernsey.co.uk/rspb-whats-on*

GOLF (126 C3) (*D4*)
You can play golf with a view of the sea at La Grande Mare Golf Club (18 holes). *Vazon Bay | Castel | tel. 01481 25 65 76 | www.lagrandemare.com*

67

THE WEST

The roar of waves: expansive Vazon Bay gives the breaking waves plenty of scope

HIKING

Visit Guernsey offers online maps and audio guides for 20 shorter hikes across the island, three in the west. *www.visit-guernsey.com/tasty-walks*

BEACHES

The beaches on the west coast are much longer and wider than those in the south – they're also equipped with car parks.

COBO BAY ★ (126 C3) (*m D3–4*)

A fantastic, very popular family beach. The sand glows white at low tide, and pink rocks rise out of the water. With pub, kiosk, chip shop, supermarket and car park.

SALINE BAY (126 C2) (*m D3*)

A perfect beach for romantics with a view of the Grandes Rocques peninsula. Take a picnic basket!

VAZON BAY (126 B–C3) (*m C–D4*)

The island's surfing centre. Atlantic rollers break against the coast, offering good conditions for pros. You can also swim in the protected pools of the Vazon Bay Battery. There's also a car park, a kiosk and a restaurant.

ENTERTAINMENT

THE ROCKMOUNT (126 C3) (*m D4*)

The sunset lounge on Cobo Bay. Only coastal roads and walls separate the terrace of the spacious pub from the beach. The food is good, the scenery with beach wall and the traffic slowed down by the barriers are quite cool.

WHERE TO STAY

COBO BAY (126 C3) (*m D4*)

The still comparatively reasonably priced

GUERNSEY

hotel has the best position on the relaxed west coast. Straight out of bed into the sea – before the excellent breakfast, you hardly need more than a minute (at low tide four or five minutes). A fine west coast restaurant with 🌿 spacious terrace – sea view with lobster. *36 rooms | Cobo Coast Road | Castel | tel. 01481 25 71 02 | www.cobobayhotel.com | Moderate*

IMPERIAL HOTEL (126 A5) (*B6*)
The hotel's pub is a meeting point for local barflies and fans of south Guernsey's live music scene – it's a place where you can quickly get chatting to the locals. *17 rooms | Portelet Harbour | tel. 01481 26 40 44 | www.imperialinguernsey.com | Budget*

WAVES (126 C3) (*D4*)
This apartment hotel with suites, studios and self-catering apartments has an ultra-modern feel and shabby chic styling. The spacious interiors offer a mixture of beach hut design and Scandinavian coolness. Many guests stay for a week. *20 rooms | Vazon Bay Road | Castel | tel. 01481 25 62 46 | www.wavesguernsey.com | Budget–Moderate*

THE NORTH

The northern part of the island is a mysterious place. Vale – the largest parish on the island with 9,600 inhabitants – isn't just awash with myths and legends, but also has ancient corridor graves that seem like windows into far-off worlds. The north also has spectacular dunes and waves almost as good for surfing as the breakers in Hawaii. Numerous Martello towers stand in the dunes around Ancresse Bay.

Besides St Peter Port, the only other small settlement that stands out is St Sampson in the north. With 8,600 inhabitants, it's the "capital" of the parish of the same name. Colourful two-storey houses and small shops are ranged along the harbour front – a typically English place with shops selling fish and chips and stores selling everyday supplies. The harbour, home to small boatyards today, still seems like a busy working place.

SIGHTSEEING

DOLMEN LE DÉHUS ★
(127 F2) (*G3*)
Once thought to be the meeting place of devils, Guernsey's corridor graves and megaliths have been extensively researched by archaeologists over the last few years. Le Déhus, built by Neolithic man 5,000 years ago, consists of one corridor, from which many side chambers branch off. An archaeologist

THE NORTH

has confirmed that Le Déhus was also sealed by its Stone Age creators – they filled the structure with limpets and then closed it off with rubble. When archaeologists opened up the grave, they found a copper dagger, ceramics and human remains. When the daylight falls in the right place, a portrait etching on the capstone is especially impressive. *Daily 9am–sunset | free entry*

LES FOUAILLAGES/LA VARDE
(127 E1–2) (*F2–3*)

An amateur archaeologist excavated around 20 dolmen here in the 19th century. The stone used in the monuments – some of it weighing 20 tonnes – was put in place before the discovery of the wheel. Several excavated graves can be found in L'Ancresse Common, the dune area in the north of Vale. Les Fouaillages, one of the most recent discoveries, is also one of the oldest monuments on the Channel Islands. From pottery shards found at the site, it's thought that the site was created between 4850 and 4250 BC. You'll find it next to the fifth hole at a golfing course above the cove Ladies' Bay.

ROUSSE TOWER (127 E1) (*F2*)
This grey granite tower was built to protect the island in the early 19th century, when it was kitted out with cannon and watchmen. It's been restored today and houses an exhibition about the history of the 15 so-called Loophole towers. Great view! *April–Oct daily 9am–sunset | free entry*

VALE CASTLE (127 F2) (*G3*)
Vale Castle was built in the 14th century. A ruin is all that remains today, but it still offers a beautiful view of the neighbouring islands of Herm and Sark. There's a big festival held here every year in August. The programme offers a varied mix of jazz, rock and hip-hop. *www.valeearthfair.org*

Royal Guernsey Golf Club: at L'Ancresse Common, you tee off between the Martello towers

GUERNSEY

FOOD & DRINK

THE BEACH HOUSE (127 E1) *(₥ F2)*
A busy, terraced beach restaurant located in Pembroke Bay. Good fish and chips, lasagne and a lobster club sandwich with a pinot grigio, also for eating at the beach. *Daily | tel. 01481 24 64 94 | Budget*

THE BEAUCETTE MARINA RESTAURANT (127 F1) *(₥ G2)*
This restaurant in the pretty Beaucette Marina serves good steak, fish and pasta. Kinda trendy. *Closed Mon | tel. 01481 24 70 66 | Moderate*

HOUMET TAVERN ☼ (127 E2) *(₥ F3)*
This restaurant in Le Grand Havre near Rousse Tower is inviting with its fantastic beach view and seafood. Generous portions, pool and billiards inside and sports TV. *Closed Sun evening | tel. 01481 24 22 14 | Moderate*

ROC SALT ☼ (127 E1) *(₥ F2)*
Directly above Ladies Bay is one of the best seafood restaurants with a view. Excellent wines. *Closed Sun evening and Mon | Mont Cuet Road | tel. 01481 24 61 29 | www.rocsalt.gg | Moderate*

INSIDER TIP ROUSSE TOWER KIOSK (127 E1) *(₥ F2)*
This busy kiosk in a restored tower at the coast sells cake, crab salad and sandwiches from May to September daily from 10am. Enjoy them on the enticing ☼ terrace with small tables where you can sit and relax with the beautiful view of the large bay of Le Grand Havre.

SHOPPING

FREESIA CENTRE (127 E2) *(₥ F3)*
The freesia and carnation grower, which sends flowers by post across Europe, shows how it works here. INSIDER TIP There is an interesting video about the time when Guernsey had countless greenhouses and was an Eldorado of flower-growing. *Route Carre | Vale*

LEISURE & SPORTS

ABSEILING
The many beaches mean numerous rocky crossings, for instance, Fort Pembroke and Port Soif. Ideal for a small test of bravado: with helmet, seatbelt and professional instruction. *Tel. 07781 13 04 03 | www.outdoorguernsey.gg*

ROYAL GUERNSEY GOLF CLUB (127 E1) *(₥ F2)*
Guernsey's best club. You can play at Ancresse Common green if you have a handicap. 18 holes. *Tel. 01481 24 65 23 | www.royalguernseygolfclub.com*

BEACHES

LADIES' BAY/GRAND HAVRE (127 E1–2) *(₥ F2–3)*
A wide, sandy, horseshoe-shaped beach that's good for swimming, even with kids. There's a car park and the Roc Salt restaurant.

PEMBROKE BAY (127 E1) *(₥ F2)*
Ideal for windsurfing, sailing and catamarans. Beautiful grassland and dunes behind the beach, and a car park with a kiosk.

PORT GRAT (127 D2) *(₥ E3)*
A small, sandy, somewhat forgotten bay in the northwest – a good place to be alone. If you walk towards the Rousse Headland you'll stumble over mussels and oysters packed in sacks to make them grow.

ST PETER PORT

PORTINFER BAY/PORT SOIF
(127 D2) *(m D–E3)*
Two small, secluded sandy beaches on the northwest coast (dunes protection area).

ENTERTAINMENT

On St Sampson harbour front there are pubs where islanders meet up who don't work in the financial sector. Namely, the *Mariners Inn:* pool, karaoke, tombolas. Happy hour for a cheap pint is from 5pm to 6pm.

WHERE TO STAY

THE BAY APARTMENTS (127 E1) *(m F2)*
In the far north, only 100 m/328 ft from the beach at Pembroke Bay, is the attractive house with various different sizes of holiday apartments. Guests can take the boat to Herm free of charge (except in July and August). Early booking is recommended! *La Jaonneuse Road | Vale | tel. 07781 14 51 29 | www.thebayguernsey.co.uk | Moderate*

PENINSULA HOTEL (127 E2) *(m F3)*
This hotel with a garden, pool and its own private beach area of the Grand Havre Bay is situated on a small peninsula. Sea view at extra cost. *99 rooms | Les Dicqs | Vale | tel. 01481 24 84 00 | www.peninsulahotelguernsey.com | Budget–Moderate*

ST PETER PORT

MAP INSIDE BACK COVER
(127 E4) *(m F5)* ★ This small capital city welcomes you with more old school flair than St Helier. Compact and with houses on steep slopes above the yacht marina, the obviously more Francophile miniature metropolis is instantly captivating.

In the small main streets with granite Victorian buildings, boutiques, jewellery shops and a few dozen international banks have set up – everything is discreet and almost understated.

St Peter Port transformed itself from a strategic harbour into a prosperous mercantile capital around the turn of the 19th century. Many fortunes were made after the British Government legalised

GUERNSEY

piracy. Around 16,500 people live in St Peter Port today. During the summer months, several thousand cruise guests also arrive daily. The large cruise ships anchor far offshore. The yacht marina is also always crowded.

SIGHTSEEING

ARCADE (U E3) (*m* e3)
This shopping arcade was built in the 1920s opposite the restored market hall, which houses a shopping mall today. Craftsmen and other businesses have set up shop behind the arcade's fine façade, which is decorated with masks, ornaments and other embellishments. The buildings themselves were built on top of deep underground shafts: large water reservoirs were created below the street level for use against fires – which would soon spread bearing in mind all the wooden floors and staircases.

INSIDER TIP BLUEBELL WOOD
(U E6) (*m* e6)
Standing at 40 cm/16 in tall and particularly common in woodlands, the bluebell

Cosmopolitan capital: St Peter Port, Guernsey's financial hotbed and exquisite residential district

ST PETER PORT

is perhaps the most popular British wildflower – an icon of spring. Guernsey has the Channel Islands' most beautiful collection of bluebells. If you venture to the upmarket residential area of Fort Field to the north of Fermain bay between the middle of April and May, you can step directly from the coastal path into a paleblue carpet of flowers. *short.travel/kai3*

Concerts and dance performances take place between 3pm and 4pm from June to September. *Mon–Sat 9.30am–5pm | free entry | Candie Road*

Hauteville House: on Guernsey, the poet and bon viveur Victor Hugo found an exile in style

CANDIE GARDENS
(U D–E2) (*d–e2*)
A statue of Victor Hugo adorns these gardens, which are located above the town. Camellias bloom in spring, hydrangeas flourish in summer, and there are views right over to Sark and Herm.

CASTLE CORNET ★
(U F3–4) (*f3–4*)
A cannon shot rings out over Castle Cornet every day at noon sharp. The castle is a dark presence between the harbour and Havelet Bay. The castle, the foundation walls of which date back to the 13th century, was originally used as a military base and a prison. It later became the Lieutenant Governor's seat, before providing a site for anti-aircraft guns during the German occupation.

GUERNSEY

As well as the *Story of Castle Cornet Museum*, there's the *Maritime Museum*, which tells the story of Guernsey's seafaring history. Military history is presented at the *Museum of the Royal Guernsey Militia*. In summer, it's worth walking through the four gardens, especially the small *herb garden*. From June to mid August, INSIDER TIP the castle becomes an open-air theatre staging popular plays, such as Romeo and Juliet and the Hunchback of Notre Dame *(tickets tel. 01481 71 22 40)*. *April–Oct daily 10am–5pm | £10.50 | www.museums.gov.gg*

GUERNSEY MUSEUM AT CANDIE (U D2) *(m d2)*

The Guernsey Museum and the ☼ Victoria Tea House sit in pride of place over Candie Gardens. The museum presents Guernsey's archaeological and historical roots with the help of pictures, displays, and artefacts. The Art Gallery displays work by local artists, including Guernsey resident Peter le Vasseur. A well-known British artist, Vasseur designed the Millennium Ark picture for the World Wide Fund for Nature and counts Beatle Ringo Starr and members of the British Royal Family among his clients. *April–Oct daily 10am–5pm, Nov/Dec and Feb/March 10am–4pm | £6.50 | www.museums.gov.gg*

THE GUERNSEY TAPESTRY (U D–E3) *(m d–e3)*

Here, a series of tapestries represent the ten parishes of Guernsey. It's interesting to note that you can recognise the older tapestries by their more muted colours. That's because plant-based dyes were used at the start – chemical colours only became part of the production process later on. *Easter–Oct Mon–Sat 10am–4.30pm, Nov–Easter Thu 11am–4pm | £5 | College Street | www.guernseytapestry.org.gg*

HAUTEVILLE HOUSE (VICTOR HUGO'S HOUSE) ★ ● (U E4) *(m e4)*

France celebrated the 210th anniversary of Victor Hugo in 2012. Hugo – poet, dramatist, bon vivant and writer of the "Hunchback of Notre Dame" and "Les Misérables" – wasn't always welcome in his homeland, however. Fleeing from Napoleon Bonaparte, he moved to Guernsey, where he lived in stylish exile in Hauteville House. The great eccentric lived in the white villa with its landscaped garden for 15 years. While there, he built a red velvet salon, painted, wrote, and collected. He wrote "Les Travailleurs de la Mer" ("Toilers of the Sea") in his study with a view towards France and the house of his beloved. It's the only one of his works that takes place on the Channel Islands. When the house, which looks like an artwork, urgently needed renovation, the French millionaire and art collector François Pinault – who earned his wealth with Gucci and Yves Saint Laurent – donated 3 million euros *(£2.7 million/$3.75 million)* for the work. *Re-opening planned in 2019 | 38 Hauteville | www.visitguernsey.com/victor-hugo, hautevillehouse.com*

ROYAL COURT (U E3) *(m e3)*

INSIDER TIP The island's Parliament with its 47 members convenes on the last Wednesday of the month in this 18th-century building. Visitors are allowed to watch from a small gallery. *Rue de Manoir | For session times: tel. 01481 72 61 61*

TOWN CHURCH (U E3) *(m e3)*

The bells in this 11th-century church strike every hour. It's so close to the Albion House pub that it once gained entry to the Guinness Book of Records. Highlights include the windows, the carved Gothic altar and the richly decorated bishop's throne.

75

ST PETER PORT

LA VALETTE UNDERGROUND MILITARY MUSEUM (U F4) (*f4*)
In this tunnel complex – which was originally used as fuel storage facility for U-boats by the Germans during Second World War – you can see exhibition pieces from the time of the occupation. *March–mid-Nov daily 10am–5pm | £6 | La Valette, opposite the Bathing Places*

VICTORIAN SHOP
(U E3) (*e3*)
Ladies in lace bonnets weigh sweets and sell violet pastilles and plant seeds in this Victorian Shop and Parlour. It's like stepping back in time, thanks to being taken over as a cultural asset by the National Trust of Guernsey. *April–Oct Tue–Sat 10am–4pm | 26 Cornet Street*

INSIDER TIP VICTORIA TOWER
(U D2) (*d2*)
Begun after Queen Victoria's 1846 visit to the island, this tower was intended as a memorial to mark the occasion. Built in the Victorian baronial style and reminiscent of a Scottish castle, the tower was probably built on the site of a Neolithic Dolmen. If you'd like to enjoy the magnificent view from a height of about 30 m/98.4 ft, ask for the key at the Guernsey Museum in Candie Gardens. *Daily 10am–4pm | free entry | short.travel/kai2*

FOOD & DRINK

CURRY ROOM (U E3) (*e3*)
The island's only five-star hotel, the Old Governor's House, is like a charming,

Small shops, short distances, cool fashion: shopping delight in St Peter Port

GUERNSEY

luxury country hotel. The two restaurants are less French than you would suppose. The *Curry Room* even serves fine Indian cuisine as though the British empire had established a culinary branch. You can also dine outdoors by the pool. *Daily | Ann's Place | tel. 01481 72 49 21 | www. theoghhotel.com | Expensive*

THE HOOK (U E3) (*e3*)
With a modern interior and a mix of sushi, seafood and steak, the restaurant by the harbour has everything. It's so trendy that booking is essential. Food is served here well after midnight! *Daily | North Plantation | tel. 01481 70 13 73 | www. thehook.gg | Moderate*

LE NAUTIQUE (U E3) (*e3*)
This warehouse-style harbour restaurant has a down-to-earth atmosphere that's loved by locals and visitors alike. Book a 🌿 table with a view of the boats. Love brought chef Günter Botzenhardt to the island, and his first-class cuisine is his way of saying thanks. He buys fish and mussels from divers and fishermen right by the front door. *Closed Saturdays | Quay Steps | tel. 01481 72 17 14 | www.lenautiquerestaurant.co.uk | Budget*

LE PETIT BISTRO (U E2) (*e2*)
Vive la France! A picture-book bistro; the cuisine is surf and turf and frogs' legs influenced by Guernsey's nature. **INSIDER TIP** From 6pm until 6.30pm in the evening, there is a three-course early bird menu for £14. *Closed Sun | 56 Lower Pollet | tel. 01481 72 50 55 | petitbistro. co.uk | Budget–Moderate*

THE SWAN INN (U E2) (*e2*)
Since being restored, this popular pub combines the ambience of its proud old age with cutting-edge service. There's also a small restaurant upstairs. Meals are cheaper than in the top restaurants, but hold their own in terms of quality. *Daily | St Julian's Avenue | tel. 01481 72 89 69 | Budget–Moderate*

THE TERRACE GARDEN CAFE 🌿 (U E3) (*e3*)
Even when the weather is not so good, it's worth rounding off the day with a delicious plate of Thai food here on the spacious terrace. There is a fabulous view over the masts in the harbour and Castle Cornet. *Daily | Cornet Street | tel. 01481 72 44 78 | www.terracegardencafe.com | Budget*

SHOPPING

Guernsey is a little more reasonable than Jersey because so far no value added tax has been introduced here. Le Pollet and the High Street invite you to stroll and enjoy window shopping. The Arcade district near the market hall is nearby.

BUCKTROUTS (U E3) (*e3*)
Picnicking on Herm's white beach? The only thing missing is the perfect accompaniment. Why not try a champagne from Veuve Clicquot Ponsardin? You can even buy it in 1.5 litre magnum bottles at Bucktrouts. *Town Church Square*

BUTTONS BOOKSHOP (U E3) (*e3*)
A large selection of literature about the Channel Islands, including books by folklore specialist Marie de Garis. *23–25 Pollet*

HIDEAWAY PATISSERIE (U E3) (*e3*)
Do you feel like sitting in one of St Peter Port's parks to enjoy a picnic? Or to find the capital's best sandwiches? This fabulous bakery on the High Street not only makes Austrian patisserie but the best Guernsey crab ciabattas. From 2pm to 5pm it gets very British, and you can

77

ST PETER PORT

Espresso or a sundowner: Christies is a popular spot from early morning to late

stay to enjoy INSIDER TIP cucumber sandwiches, Scones with jam and rich Guernsey cream are served. It's probably best to give dinner a miss ... *Daily | Le Pollet*

LITTLE GINGER EN PROVENCE
(U E3) (*e3*)
Is there Guernsey chic? In this pretty boutique of an elective Guernsey islander from Paris you can discover Channel Island fashion with a French twist. The best thing is that the clothing, bags and accessories are produced INSIDER TIP with sustainable and fair trade ideals in mind. Many items are also vegan. *8 The Pollet*

LEISURE & SPORTS

BEAU SÉJOUR CENTRE (U D–E1) (*d–e1*)
A pool, fitness suites, squash, tennis, badminton, a bar and restaurants and roller-skating for the kids. *Daily 7am–11pm | Amherst Road | tel. 01481 74 72 00 | www.beausejour.gg*

ISLAND RIB VOYAGES (U F2) (*f2*)
At first, it sounds too fast and loud, but it's totally fabulous to travel from St Julian's pier to Sark and Herm or to the cliffs and caves. The one-hour trip is adapted for dolphin spotting and it stops for seals. *£30 | www.islandribvoyages.com*

THEMED WALKING TOURS
Annette Henry leads walking tours year-round: her ghost tours are just one example. During the darker months, these gruesome evenings also include dinner (*£27*). Gill Girard also offers tours on various topics. *Tel. 01481 26 37 55 | www.annettehenrytours.gg; www.gillgirardtourguide.com*

ENTERTAINMENT

You'll be spoiled for choice with the range of local bands, classical concerts and jam sessions on offer. Bands come from Jersey and southern England at the weekend. Find out more about live acts and clubbing at: *www.guernseygigs.com*

BARBADOS BEACH CLUB
(U E2) (*e2*)
Relaxed club style, dance floors, but also lounges to sit and talk. Vibrant and not just intended for young people. *Lower Pollet | www.barbadosguernsey.com*

THE BOATHOUSE (U E3) (*e3*)
In pole position by the harbour, a fantastic spot with great menu that will even please vegetarians. In early evening,

GUERNSEY

people sit here with a beer or cider before dinner right by the harbour. *Victoria Pier*

CHRISTIES (U E3) (📖 e3)
At the front, a French bistro with Art Deco design, and at the back a 🌿 popular restaurant with a small terrace (booking essential!) that overlooks St Peter Port harbour. Guernsey locals meet here for a drink after work. *Le Pollet | tel. 01481 72 66 24 | www.christies.gg*

THE DOG HOUSE (127 E4) (📖 E5)
There are live bands several times a week, you can also get a good meal or watch sports on TV. The local music scene – ranging from folk rock to indie – is well represented. Better reserve a table. *Rohais | tel. 01481 72 13 02 | www.doghouse.gg*

LASKA (U E3) (📖 e3)
Fancy a cocktail or mocktail (from £9)? This right address! A younger clientele, stylish interiors, the music isn't too loud. Open from 4pm. *South Esplanade*

WHERE TO STAY

BEST WESTERN HOTEL DE HAVELET (U E4) (📖 e4)
A tasteful hotel with a view of Castle Cornet and the harbour. *34 rooms | Havelet | tel. 01481 72 21 99 | www.dehavelet guernsey.com | Moderate*

THE MARTON GUEST HOUSE (U D4) (📖 d4)
Good value accommodation with a park on the southwestern edge of the centre. *28 rooms | Les Vardes | tel. 01481 72 09 71 | www.martonguesthouse.com | Budget*

THE OLD GOVERNMENT HOUSE HOTEL 🌿 (U E3) (📖 e3)
A lovely old estate complete with attractively renovated rooms, a spa, a bar, restaurants and a great deal of enchanting little touches. You'll feel like you're staying with wealthy relatives. *68 rooms | Ann's Place | tel. 01481 72 49 21 | www.theoghhotel.com | Expensive*

LES ROCQUETTES (127 E4) (📖 E5)
A hotel whose age has been charmingly preserved and carefully upgraded. A pool, car park, lively bar, spacious bedrooms and comfortable lounges. Feels more like a four- than three-star hotel. *50 rooms | Les Gravees | tel. 01481 72 21 46 | www.lesrocquettesguernsey.com | Moderate*

ST GEORGE'S GUEST HOUSE (U E1) (📖 e1)
Only a few minutes' walk from the harbour by the water (🌿 rooms with a sea view are available at a premium). Clean, friendly and with a good breakfast. There is almost no competition in St Peter Port for this price bracket. *20 rooms | St George's Esplanade | tel. 01481 72 10 27 | www.stgeorges-guernsey.com | Budget*

ZIGGURAT (U E3) (📖 e3)
Ziggurat means a pyramid with platforms – the 14-room hotel is arranged in this style over several floors and the design (with small, but excellent rooms) is reminiscent of the ambience in the eastern Mediterranean, only you are overlooking the roof-tops of St Peter Port from the balcony. *5 Constitution Steps | tel. 01481 72 30 08 | www.hotelziggurat.com | Budget–Moderate*

INFORMATION

GUERNSEY TOURIST INFORMATION (U E3) (📖 e3)
North Esplanade | tel. 01481 72 35 52 | www.visitguernsey.com

ALDERNEY

Why visit Alderney? Island lovers go simply because it's there. Other people visit because it's completely different from its siblings. The small island, weighing in at 3 mi² isn't an obvious Treasure Island like Guernsey, but it has its own particular attractions.

The atmosphere is more relaxed than on Guernsey which is 32 km/19.9 mi away. But between Normandy and Alderney, 15 km/9.3 mi away, is Europe's fiercest tidal current: "The Race" creates up to twelve knots! Alderney's shipwrecks are silent evidence. Currently, the prospect of tidal electricity is being evaluated, since the Channel Islands are in the middle of over ten per cent of the world's tidal power. Alderney is already earning good money from a different power: international Internet lottery is a virtual resource on the island because no taxes are levied here for registered companies nor on profit. The island is upgrading its infrastructure thanks to its concessions.

The island's attractions for visitors are its cosiness and its large number of military fortifications – fans of wartime architecture easily double the island's 2,000-strong population in the summer. The English began fortifying the island during the Napoleonic Wars, a process continued by the German occupiers during Second World War. While the Victorians mainly built in the island granite, the Germans used concrete. Regular visitors to Alderney, many of whom stay at the large campsite, like to stroll

Photo: Braye Bay

An island for "hobbyists": British eccentricity reigns on the northernmost of the five islands

through the bunkers, enjoy the sandy bays, watch the acrobatic gannets dive for fish, and appreciate the millions of coastal flowers and wild orchids that bloom here.

Fans of Alderney view the island as a slice of paradise, and the perfect place to while away the time with an eccentric hobby. In this spirit, why not take a ride on the small island railway? The train service is entirely run by volunteers – as are the museum, the shipwreck diving service, the cinema and the lifeboats. It can seem at times that Alderney is run almost entirely by an army of keen enthusiasts.

Despite this appearance, there are some jobs of a more serious nature. Such roles include the elected President of the States of Alderney and the ten presidential deputies. From 2 July 1940 until 16 May 1945, the German Wehrmacht occupied the island. The population fled shortly before they arrived, with the majority going to Scotland. The island's 370 or so Alderney cows were taken to

Guernsey. While on the island, the Nazis set up the Sylt concentration camp. Prisoners and forced workers had to lay 30,000 mines on the coast and build around 50 concrete bunkers, many of which survive today. The Victorian and Nazi fortifications make Alderney a little like an abandoned fortress.

Thanks to the warming effects of the Gulf Stream, plants flourish here, creating a more peaceful atmosphere. A particularly large number of yellow flowers cover the island in a spectacular display from spring through till autumn. While up to 1,000 wild varieties of plant flourish, including 200 that bloom in winter, many gardens feature Mediterranean and even Pacific species.

While respecting the memory of its victims, the islanders deal with the appalling history of the Nazi occupation with a typical pinch of British humour: the Fawlty Towers-inspired sign over the bar of the Marais Hall pub ("Don't mention the war"), displayed by the German owners, was just one example. But people have come to terms with the war now.

SIGHTSEEING

ALDERNEY RAILWAY ★
(128 B–C1) (*m* N–O 1–2)

Alderney is the only Channel Island still to have a functioning railway. The route runs 3 km/1.9 mi from the Mannez Granite Quarry to Braye Harbour. It made its first trip in 1847, and was used to transport granite for building the Victorian forts and the breakwater. At the end of 1911, the train fell from the breakwater into the sea – fortunately without loss of life. "Elizabeth", today's diesel train, has been in service since 1985. In 2001, the old train carriages, which had fallen victim to corrosion brought on by the salty atmosphere, were replaced with two aluminium carriages from the London Underground. On Sundays in July and August, an extra mini train travels

As fabulously retro and nostalgic as the entire island: the railway on Alderney

ALDERNEY

about 400 m/1,300 ft on a narrower track – it's great fun for kids. *Easter and May–Sept Sun, July/Aug Sat and Sun 2.30pm and 3.30pm | £6 return ticket | www.alderneyrailway.com*

ALDERNEY SOCIETY MUSEUM ⭐
(128 B2) (*M2*)

This enterprising museum started life as the private collection of the potter Peter Arnold. The glass cases display artefacts relating to the history of the island. You can learn about the German occupation, about Alderney's possible Roman past, and about the equipment taken from the many ships that have run aground in the island's dangerous waters over the centuries. The museum's highlights include finds from an Elizabethan shipwreck and the diary entries of forced labourers held on Alderney during the German occupation. The museum often expands its collection with objects found on the island. *April–Oct daily 10–12am, Mon–Fri also 2.30pm–4.30pm | £3 | Lower High Street | St Anne | www.alderneysociety.org*

BRAYE HARBOUR (128 B1) (*M1–2*)
This small, bustling harbour is protected by a long sea wall. The Victorian garrisons built the breakwater in 1847, 870 m/2,854 ft of which still survive today. It's worth taking a stroll along the wall in the morning or the evening – anglers should also take their rods, as it's a good spot for fishing. Alderney is known for its large conger eels, though the largest marine mammal to visit Braye Bay is a plankton-eating basking shark that grows to a length of up to 13 m/42.7 ft. A row of multi-storey terraced houses with pastel coloured facades is a remnant from the time when the harbour was a more important location than the island "metropolis" of St Anne.

CINEMA ● (128 B2) (*M2*)
Alderney's cinema has only one piece of portable projection equipment. This means that every film shown includes a break: the screen goes blank while the projectionist changes the reels. During the interval, the 90-strong audience decamps across the street for a beer in The Georgian House. A bell calls the filmgoers back for the second half. The cinema's speakers are real museum pieces. *£6 | Victoria Street | St Anne*

LONGIS BAY AND LONGIS NATURE RESERVE (128 C1) (*N–O2*)
This beautiful swimming bay in the southeast is topped by a powerful – but somehow almost dainty looking – Nazi construction. The wall, built to defend against tanks, follows the 800 m/2,625 ft stretch of sandy beach and provides the best wind protection on Alderney. Despite the concrete's

---

MARCO POLO HIGHLIGHTS

⭐ **Alderney Railway**
Eccentric railway fun → p. 82

⭐ **Alderney Society Museum**
Showcasing the island's eventful past → p. 83

⭐ **Victorian Forts**
Granite defences on the coast → p. 84

⭐ **Wildlife Trust Bunker**
Watch the flight manoeuvres of the sea birds from this old Wehrmacht bunker → p. 85

⭐ **Pub crawl**
An alcohol-fuelled trip from pub to pub through St Anne, Alderney's "capital" → p. 86

Island idyll: St Anne's graveyard and church

ST ANNE (128 B2) *(M2)*

Situated on a hill in the centre of Alderney, this town seems like a metropolis on such a small island. The rustic granite houses and uneven cobblestones are reminiscent of towns in the close-by Normandy. The Victoria Street shopping strip forms the centre of St Anne, while the town's church and graveyard are worth a visit. You can buy Alderney stamps in the Alderney Post Office *(18 Victoria Street | www.guernseystamps.com)*. The stamps – featuring birds, mushrooms and flowers – make nice souvenirs.

VICTORIAN FORTS ★

The English built a dozen impressive coastal forts on Alderney between 1840 and 1865. The fortifications were designed to quash Napoleon Bonaparte's dreams of invasion. Most of the forts can only be viewed from the outside today: some are privately owned, others are made unreachable by the swell of the tides, and some of the ruins are dangerous to enter.

The south wing and the Moroccan Room of *Fort Corblets* (128 C1) *(O1)* in Corblets Bay can be rented as holiday *(from £880/week | www.fortcorblets.co.uk)*. *Fort Tourgis* (128 A2) *(M2)*, west of Crabby Bay, is the island's largest fort. No new purpose has yet been found for this romantic stronghold. *Fort Doyle* (128 B1) *(M2)*, in contrast, is used by the island's boxing club.

Fort Clonque (128 A2) *(L2)* now belongs to the British Landmark Trust and must be one of the most fantastic hostels in the whole of Great Britain. Adventure-hungry groups of up to 13 people can take up residence in the stronghold's spartan rooms (4 nights from £775). There is a genuine drawbridge, a flag pole (naturally!), iron beds, a lounge with an open fire and a vast kitchen. The

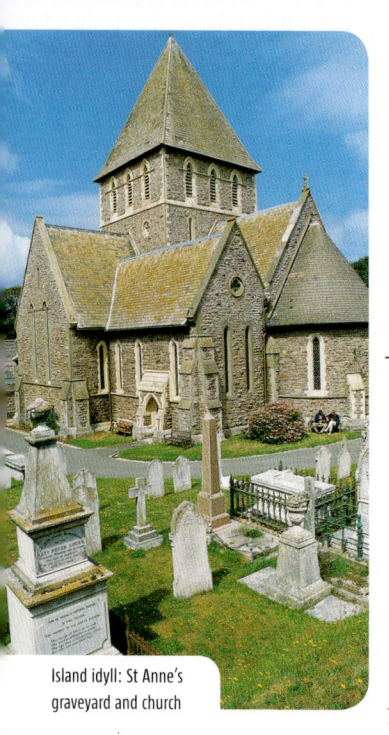

appalling history, the wall is a very relaxing place today: find the right partner, grab some wine, and lean against the warm concrete in the evening. The Nunnery, a former military building, stands at the bay's western end. Numerous Roman artefacts have been found here, suggesting that they once had an outpost on the island.

The enterprising Wildlife Trust has established a hide for watching birds behind Longis Bay. It's a particularly good place for observing feathered goings on in the 371-acre *Longis Nature Reserve*. The star of the plant world is a small orchid (orchis morio); several thousand specimens of this spring-flowering, purpole bloom are found on the island of Alderney alone. *www.alderneywildlife.org*

ALDERNEY

sea thunders against the foundation walls, and the walkway over the causeway is sometimes flooded for hours at a stretch when the sea is violent. *www.landmarktrust.org.uk*

BIRD ISLANDS (128 A2–3) *(M L3)*
The west coast of Alderney and its offshore reefs and islands were dubbed a Ramsar wetland worthy of conservation for water and wading birds. Over 6,000 pairs of gannets breed in *Telegraph Bay* and on the *Les Etacs* and *Ortac* rock formations in the summer. Puffins (until mid-June) and storm petrels also make the journey to the island of *Burhou*. Their breeding sites can be visited (but not accessed) on a boat tour or observed through a webcam. *Information about boat trips: tel. 01481 82 29 35 | alderneywildlife.org; tel. 07781 10 08 29 | www.alderneygiftbox.com*

WILDLIFE TRUST BUNKER ★ ●
(128 B2) *(M M3)*
This south coast bunker has been converted into an information centre for anyone interested in the flora and fauna of the island. The former generator room is filled with informative wall charts. You can watch gliding gannets, acrobatic fulmar and hunting black-backed gulls from the parapets once used for shooting and military observation. Binoculars are provided. *Daily 8am–sunset | free entry | Val du Saou | www.alderneywildlife.org*

FOOD & DRINK

INSIDER TIP ▶ BRAYE CHIPPY
(128 B1) *(M M–N2)*
This simple chip shop at the harvour is where the islanders go when they want to eat good fish and chips. *Daily | Braye Harbour | tel. 01481 82 34 75 | Budget*

BUMPS BAR & BISTRO
(128 B1) *(M M–N2)*
Protein, protein, protein: steaks and lobster served right next to the harbour, but you can get tapas as well. *Closed Wed | Braye Harbour | tel. 01481 82 31 97 | Moderate*

GEORGIAN HOUSE
(128 B2) *(M M2)*
A good culinary destination that's recently been restyled. There's a great atmosphere, an international menu, and the customers are the island's Who's Who. *Daily | Victoria Street | St Anne | tel. 01481 82 24 71 | Moderate*

MARAIS HALL (128 B2) *(M M2)*
A cosy, traditional pub. Visitors and locals squeeze in tight together to enjoy the tasty steak and lobster. *Daily | Marais Square | St Anne | tel. 01481 82 26 83 | Budget*

LEISURE & SPORTS

GOLF (128 B1–2) *(M N2)*
This 9-hole course on the edge of St Anne is open to visitors. *Tel. 01481 82 28 35*

LOW BUDGET

You can learn about the sometimes tragic, sometimes comic history of the island during a two-hour bus trip from St Anne for just £15. *Tue–Thu 2pm*

Save cash by staying at the island's only campsite, *Saye Beach Camping (tent £7.50/person | www.sayebeachcamping.co.uk)* at the beautiful Saye Bay.

INSIDER TIP ▶ **HEDGEHOGSPOTTING**
At night, the island reveals a curious secret: a quarter of all Alderney's hedgehogs are blond. It's thought that an escaped pet bought from Harrods in London is to thank for the island's unusually high proportion of these rare, light-prickled creatures. You can see them at night if you venture out with a torch. You also encounter bats on the guided nightlife tour. *Wed | tel. 01481 82 29 35*

MEDITATION CENTRE LA TRIGALE
(128 B2) (*M2*)
On Alderney, wellness is practised through meditation. The small centre in a beautiful garden with Buddhist motifs offers half-hour sessions with a tutor – and afterwards there is tea and coffee. *7, La Trigale | tel. 07781 42 66 10*

CYCLING
Bikes are a good way to get round Alderney. Hire shops are in St Anne *(rental from £11/day, e-bike £20). www.cycleandsurf.co.uk; www.automotionalderney.com*

HIKING
You can easily get around the small island in a day on foot. The most beautiful routes are the coastal path in the west and the bay route between Saye Bay and Longis Bay in the northeast.

BEACHES

The best swimming beaches can be found at *Braye Bay* (128 B1) (*N2*). *Saye Bay* has a campsite and is the best spot for building sandcastles (128 B–C1) (*N1*). For bodyboarding, check out *Corblets Bay* (128 C1) (*N–O1*). *Longis Bay* and *Arch Bay* (128 C1) (*N–O2*) are great for the kids. *Saline Bay* (128 A–B1) (*M2*) is beautiful and nice for exploring, but swimming is too dangerous. The rocks of *Clonque Beach* (128 A2) (*M2*) are great for discovering starfish, sea anemones, crabs and a variety of shrimp.

ENTERTAINMENT

Alderney's nightlife is astonishing, considering the island's small size. Some english visitors come here just for the ★ *pub crawl*. Meet the locals at the *Divers Inn* down at the harbour, then walk a few hundred feet into town and left at the Fish & Last restaurant to the *Harbour Lights* in Newtown. It's worth taking the 20-minute walk down into St Anne because the pubs on Victoria Street and the High Street buzz in the summer. There's always something going on in the *Campania* and the *Coronation*. You can have a quieter meal and a drink in *Marais Hall*.

WHERE TO STAY

BIRD OBSERVATORY (128 C1) (*N2*)
Sleep next to bird watchers in a hostel

ALDERNEY

in a small, Roman fort. You can also try ringing the migratory birds. A group experience at the heart of nature! *Tel. 07815 54 91 91 | www.alderneybirdobservatory.org | Budget*

BON JOUR GUEST HOUSE (128 B2) *(M2)*
Good value accommodation in the middle of the charming "capital" of St Anne. The B&B can be booked with half-board. 7 rooms | 16 High Street | tel. 01481 82 21 52 | Budget

BRAYE BEACH HOTEL (128 B1) *(M2)*
The largest and finest hotel on this small island. It combines modern comfort with a classy restaurant and there's a cinema for stormy days. *27 rooms | Braye Street | tel. 01481 82 43 00 | www.brayebeach.com | Expensive*

FARM COURT GUEST HOUSE (128 B2) *(M2)*
Extremely cosy – the whitewashed stone walls contrast with the modern lighting and the carefully selected old furniture. The paintings are the landlord's. *7 rooms | Les Mouriaux | tel. 01481 82 20 75 | www.farmcourt-alderney.co.uk | Moderate–Expensive*

VILLA MONDRIAN (128 B2) *(M2)*
This white villa is designed in the architectural style of Bauhaus, located

The rocky Clonque Bay on Alderney's north coast: a playground for crabs, starfish and prawns

on the northern edge of St Anne. The four modern rooms are reminiscent of the colour palette of the painter whom the villa is named after. With terraces, without breakfast – and nice and private. *Fontaine David | tel. 07911 72 37 03 | www.villamondrian.com | Moderate*

INFORMATION

TOURIST INFORMATION CENTRE (128 B2) *(M2)*
51 Victoria Street | tel. 01481 82 23 33 | www.visitalderney.com

HERM & SARK

The two islands are partially governed by Guernsey and lie to the east of their mother island, but they feel completely different!

Victor Hugo, who was allowed to travel to Sark during his exile on Guernsey, described the island as a "fairy-tale castle, full of wonder". Sark's defiant Atlantic cliffs make it look as inaccessible as an enchanted fortress, while the much smaller Herm attracts visitors with its South Sea island feel. Both can be reached by ferry from St Peter Port on Guernsey – making them exciting day-trip destinations.

Driving cars is frowned upon on both islands, and cycling is a no-no on Herm. Inhabitants get around with tractors, by horse and trap or by quad bike (on Herm). Just spending an active day at walking pace and getting an insight into two very different worlds is reason enough to sail to these islands.

HERM

At 0.8 mi^2, Herm is the smallest of the islands and is inhabited by just 60 people. There's a hotel and a few pubs and restaurants serving its 65,000 visitors per year. There's also a school for children up to 10 years old.

The presence of a school on the island is down to the island's last tenants, the Wood family (1980–2008) from New Zealand, who welcomed couples with children to settle on the island.

No cars, no traffic jams, no noise: Sark is dreamily romantic, and Herm is a slice of paradise

Not much has changed for holidaymakers since the New Zealanders – whose patriarch, Peter Wood, lies in a small mausoleum on Herm – sold the last 40 years of their lease agreement to a foundation in 2008. As the contract states, Herm has to remain a beautiful place for holidays, just as it was before. During summer, about 100 employees give Herm a multicultural atmosphere. Gardeners make sure Herm looks its floral best and a governor supervises the seven wells and the diesel generators. A dowser is called on to discover new springs. The small village forms the touristic heart of Herm, and includes the White House Hotel, set amid lawns and flowerbeds filled with Mediterranean and Pacific plants, and several pubs and souvenir shops.

Outside this small settlement, there's nothing except the island's magnificent beaches, which you can walk around in two to three hours. If you walk to the centre of the island, you'll come across the remains of Neolithic megaliths and tombs and a beautifully restored chapel

HERM

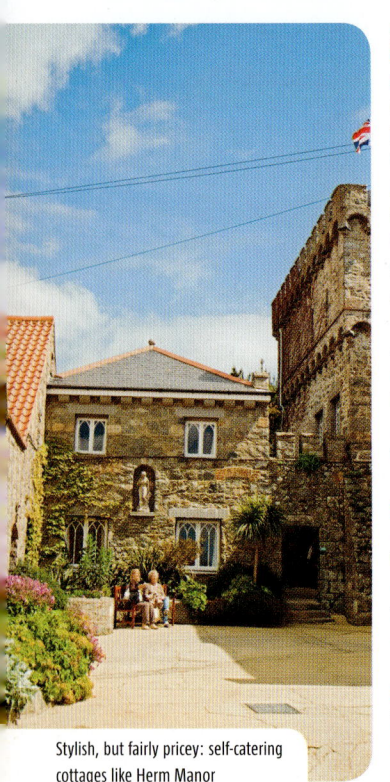

Stylish, but fairly pricey: self-catering cottages like Herm Manor

dating back to the time of the Norman monks who already lived here 1,400 years ago.

FERRY

The tidal range requires two landing places: Herm Harbour at high tide, and the Rosaire Steps when the sea is out. The 20-minute journey over to the island *(regular trips from 8.30am | £13.50)* begins in St Peter Port's harbour. The ticket office *(May–Sept daily 8am–5.15pm)* is on the Weighbridge and provides an extra landing spot. *Information: tel. 01481 721379 | www.traveltrodent.com*

SIGHTSEEING

LE MANOIR (MANOR HOUSE)
(126 A1) (*J4*)

Prince Gebhard Lebrecht Blücher von Wahlstatt bought the island in 1891. He remodelled the manor house and the chapel, giving them their noble facades. As he had been born in Prussia, he was banished from the island after the outbreak of WW1. The estate is now the residence of the island tenants and isn't open to visitors. The building is topped by a mighty tower. The islanders' cottages, the school, the chapel and holiday homes are scattered around the house.

POINT SAUZEBOURGE
(126 A2) (*J4*)

The island's southernmost point rises out of the sea at a height of up to 70 m/229.7 ft, giving an excellent view of the private island of Jethou.

ST TUGUAL'S CHAPEL (126 A1) (*J4*)
This small chapel dates back to the 11th century. The Wood family immortalised Herm's beaches, cows and pine trees in the stained-glass windows. Their grave is in the small cemetery in front of the chapel.

FOOD & DRINK

MERMAID PUB (126 A1) (*J4*)
Serves typic pub food, from chilli con carne to baked potatoes. In addition, barbecues in the courtyard and often live concerts in summer. *Daily | tel. 01481 710170 | Budget*

SHIP BAR (126 A1) (*J4*)
A maritime bar with snacks and five o'clock tea by the fire. *Daily | tel. 01481 722159 | Budget*

HERM & SARK

WHITE HOUSE HOTEL RESTAURANT ☼ (126 A1) (*J4*)
Views of the harbour, the sunsets, and the lights of Guernsey combined with good cuisine and a wide selection of wines. *Daily | tel. 01481 72 2159 | Moderate*

BEACHES

BELVOIR BAY ☼ (126 B1) (*J–K4*)
The crescent-shaped Belvoir Bay lies on the east coast. The swell of the sea and the secluded beach may well make you wish you never had to leave. You can see Normandy, 40 km/24.9 mi away. *Café*

SHELL BEACH ★ (126 A1) (*J3–4*)
This heavenly beach with a summer café and a sea that glints turquoise in the sun is the real highlight of the island. The fine, powdery sand and the numerous varieties of shells found along the tide line could be straight out of the Caribbean. Check out the informative INSIDER TIP brochure "Fifty Sea Shells from Herm Island" at one of the beach kiosks if you want to find out more.

WHERE TO STAY

SEAGULL CAMPSITE ☼
(126 A1) (*J4*)
A good alternative for families: set up your tent on the summit of Herm's "mountain" and enjoy panoramic views of the sea. You don't even have to carry equipment – a well appointed tent for families costs just under £265 a week, if you have your own tents, it's £11 pp. *Tel. 01481 72 23 77 | www.herm.com/camping*

SELFCATERING COTTAGES
(126 A1) (*J4*)
20 pretty refuges perfect for getting away from it all, including ☼ Upper *Belvoir Cottage* and the white *Fisherman's Cottage* with its own beach. A house for four to six people costs from £880 per week in the summer. *Tel. 01481 72 23 77 | www.herm.com/holiday-cottages*

WHITE HOUSE HOTEL
(126 A1–2) (*J4*)
Fluttering flags, hydrangeas in the garden, and deckchairs on the perfect lawn – this is very British and full of style. Half-board and from May to October only! *40 rooms | tel. 01481 72 2159 | www.herm.com/hotel | Moderate*

INFORMATION

TOURISTENINFORMATION
(126 A1) (*J4*)
At the harbour | tel. 01481 75 00 00 | www.herm.com

MARCO POLO HIGHLIGHTS

★ **Shell Beach**
Herm meets the Caribbean: fine sand with white seashells
→ p. 91

★ **La Coupée**
Caught between heaven and earth, this vertiginous ridge with a view connects Sark with Little Sark → p. 93

★ **La Seigneurie**
A rose garden, a hedge maze, and magnificent blooms – Sark's sensory feast for flower lovers
→ p. 94

★ **La Sablonnerie**
A country hotel in an old Sark cottage. Not staying overnight? Take a seat in the tea garden
→ p. 97

SARK

The island is 2.1 mi² in size, and rises at 110 m/361 ft high above the sea.

Since the 16th century, the crown territory of Sark, which belonged to the States of Guernsey, was governed by a hereditary Seigneur. The island head governed 600 adults in feudal style and was chairman of a kind of island council where the 40 landowners controlled their own fate. Since 2008, a new system is in place: in 1993, the Barclay brothers, the billionaire owners of London's Ritz Hotel as well as newspapers, bought the island of Brecqhou that belongs to Sark. They renovated it to a private castle with garden. Then, they tackled Sark and with the help of European court rulings they cancelled the feudal customs. The result was general elections from 2008. Half of the 28 governmental offices were elected as well as the 14 seats in control of the landowners. By acquiring the lease – it is impossible to purchase crown territory – the Barclays now control about a quarter of Sark and transformed agricultural land into vineyards. They gave these up again in 2017, as Sark planned to levy taxes on alcohol. 25 jobs were lost. The atmosphere on the island is very tense – the residents are waiting for the billionaires' next chess move under the guise of democracy.

Sark's tensions are hidden from weekend visitors, unless they chat to the carriage drivers who drive the ferry tourists from Sark over the exposed causeway *La Coupée* to Little Sark. Only tractors and hire bicycles travel on the untarmacked island plateau without street lighting. Many people go on foot, strolling over the "Avenue" with shops, a post office, boutiques, banks (no cash machine!). Day-trippers spend a dream day in a wilderness tamed by the cottages, gardens and small woodlands with continual fabulous views over the rest of the world. Sark still seems as if it's from a different era. There are only two farmers left on Sark. The milk from their Guernsey cows (the only variety allowed here) are used to produce the creamy ice creams and chocolates on sale in shops on the island. The use of chemical fertilisers is forbidden in order to protect the water table.

Once upon a time, Sark was constantly popping up in the media because of the 25,000 or so "shell" corporations that took up residence on the island. Fax machines and modems could be seen in barns and greenhouses. However, limitations have been imposed on such companies.

FERRY

The 50-minute crossing (regularly from 8am; severely limited service in winter) begins on the Pier of the Sark Shipping Company in St Peter Port and ends in Sark's Maseline Harbour. Information: *Tel. 01481 72 40 59 | www.sarkshipping.gg | £29.35 return, £24.50 at 8am.*

SIGHTSEEING

CREUX HARBOUR (128 C5) (*M* N6)
This harbour, a mooring spot for fishing boats and yachts, lies near Maseline Harbour, the main port on the island. The two are connected by a tunnel. Decorated boats cross here during the Sark Water Carnival in summer.

GOULIOT CAVES (128 B4–5) (*M* M6)
Sark and Brecqhou are separated by the Gouliot Passage. The caves here, home to delicate sea anemones, can only be visited at low tide.

LITTLE SARK (128 B5–6) (*M* M7)
The cliffs fall down steeply into the sea

HERM & SARK

at ⭐ 🌿 *La Coupée*. This narrow natural dam separates Little Sark from the main island. It's a great spot for enjoying far-reaching views of the bays. It's also the gateway to an enchanted world of wild spring daffodils, towering blackberry hedges and old cottages. It's not easy to stand up here when there's a stiff breeze blowing. Cyclists and horse and carriage passengers have to dismount before crossing the narrow isthmus, first covered in concrete by German prisoners of war in 1945. Before that, it was a matter of clinging on to the railings built in 1909. In 1835, Sark experienced a silver rush. The mines employed some 80 workers and the silver was exported from Port Gorey in the southwest of the island. The refinery was shut down in 1847, but the overgrown ruins of its tower and chimney still stand today. The tide fills the **INSIDER TIP** *Venus Pool* on Little Sark's southern tip: enjoy swimming and diving in this popular 5 m-/16.4 ft-deep rock pool.

MASELINE HARBOUR (128 C4) (*N6*)

The construction of Sark's deep-water port was only completed in 1949, its construction having been interrupted by Second World War. Ferries anchor here, luggage and wares are unloaded, and visitors go through the tunnel to the small courtyard before being driven into the village or going over Harbour Hill on foot (a small path runs parallel to the road).

POINT ROBERT (128 C4) (*N6*)

The lighthouse, built in 1912, stands high over the east coast. You can climb up the 🌿 cliffs right behind the building and enjoy a panoramic view all the way to Maseline Harbour.

Carriage on La Coupée: public transport on Sark is still measured in HP and not kW

SARK

PRISON (128 B4–5) *(M N6)*
The Constable and the Vingtenier guard this tiny two-cell prison. The first female constable started work in 2003. The longest stretch an inmate can spend here is 48 hours. It's never yet happened, and any serious offences would be punished in Guernsey.

SARK OCCUPATION & HERITAGE MUSEUM (128 B4–5) *(M N6)*
This museum in Rue Lucas focuses on the history of the island and the German occupation. The small museum of the Société Sercquaise is nearby on the high street, and lovingly deals with Sark's nature and archaeology. *Summer: Mon–Sat 2pm–4.30pm | free entry | Rue Lucas*

LA SEIGNEURIE ⭐ (128 B4) *(M M6)*
The beautiful country manor was the official residence of the Seigneur since 1730 – for the first time it is leased to someone who has sympathetically restored it. A genuine gem are the expansive walled gardens and the artistic dovecote which is typical of the Channel Islands (keeping doves was a privilege of the Seigneur until 2007). *April–Oct daily 10am–5pm | £4*

ST PETER'S CHURCH (128 B4) *(M N6)*
The island's Anglican church was built for the very low price of £1,000 in 1820. The old Sark families – the island tenants – reserve their seats in the carved church pews with cushions embroidered with their coats of arms.

WINDMILL (128 B5) *(M N6)*
Built in 1571 on the island's highest point (110 m/361 ft), this is the second-oldest mill in the British Isles. Once used to process Sark's corn, it fell out of use for a long time, and the timbers slowly rotted. It has now been restored at great cost by the islanders, but visits are not permitted. The oldest building inscription on the island can be found on the northern door lintel – carved in 1571 and harking back to the time of the grain monopoly held by the Queen's liege, Helier de Carteret. The German Wehrmacht removed the top of the mill during Second World War to turn it into a viewing platform.

WINDOW IN THE ROCK ●/PORT DU MOULIN ☀ (128 B4) *(M M6)*
You can reach Port du Moulin beach with its beautiful rock formation by walking down a short footpath and descending some steps to the west of the Seigneurie. The yellow flowering gorse creeps over the rocks, and rock pennywort grows upright in the niches. Just before the steps lead to the bay, the path forks off to the Window in the Rock, a large rock opening that frames the view to the west magnificently. You can easily make out Herm and Guernsey. The remains of a rope winch date back to the time when Sark's farmers pulled seaweed up the rocks to use as fertiliser on their fields.

FOOD & DRINK

HATHAWAYS (128 B4) *(M M6)*
This restaurant with its terrace directly adjacent to the gardens of the Seigneurie is an ideal and popular lunch spot. The ingredients come fresh from the sea

LOW BUDGET

Camping is the best bet for budget accommodation on Sark (from £9/person). The two simple campsites are called *La Valette (tel. 01481 83 22 02)* and *Pomme de Chien (tel. 01481 83 23 16). www.sark.info*

HERM & SARK

An elegant "Seat of Government": La Seigneurie mansion and rose garden

and the island and are then turned into dishes with global appeal: there's tapas, salads, couscous, crabs with fennel, and lots of seafood. Sole complaint: the cappuccino leaves room for improvement. *Daily | Seigneurie Gardens | tel. 01481 832208 | www.laseigneuriegardens.com/hathaways.html | Budget*

LA SABLONNERIE (128 B5) (*M7*)
Fancy fresh lobster with an orange or light champagne sauce? And what about field fresh Sark potatoes with al dente vegetables? Then come and dine in magnificent style at La Sablonnerie. Meet in the cosy bar for a cocktail first before dining in the best restaurant on the island! The tea garden is open after lunch. The charismatic chef, Elizabeth Perré, turned down the lease from the Barclays. *Daily | Little Sark | tel. 01481 832061 | www.sablonneriesark.com | Expensive*

SHOPPING

CARAGH CHOCOLATES
(128 B5) (*M7*)
What's perhaps the smallest chocolatier in the world uses Belgian chocolate and the creamy milk of Guernsey cows to make delicious souvenirs, ranging from chocolate sea horses to champagne truffles, cherry liqueur pralines and vanilla hearts. *North of La Coupée | www.caraghchocolates.com*

LORRAINES POTTERY
(128 B4–5) (*N6*)
Pottery, earthenware and silverware from Sark. *The Avenue | www.sarkpottery.com*

95

SARK

LEISURE & SPORTS

BOAT TOURS
Sea bird expert George Guille offers three-hour boat tours. You'll learn a lot about Sark's wild coast and can you can watch puffins, guillemots and maybe even a dolphin. *Tel. 01481 83 21 07 | approx. £25 per person*

BIKE RENTAL
A suitable form of transport – book ahead in the summer! From £6 per day. *A to B Cycles (near the Mermaid Tavern | tel. 01481 83 28 44 | atobcycles.com); Avenue Cycle Hire (The Avenue | tel. 01481 83 21 02 | www.avenuecyclessark.co.uk)*

INSIDER TIP ▸ GARDEN WALKS
Afternoon tea in a cottage garden: many islanders open their gardens up to visitors in the summer. Tours start at 2pm on Fridays at the Island Hall and end with a spot of tea in the last garden you visit. *£5*

HORSE AND CARRIAGE TRIPS ●
A horse and carriage is clearly the nicest way to explore the island. They wait for passengers at the intersection of La Colinette and Rue Lucas. *90 min £14 | tel. 01481 83 20 27 and 01481 83 21 35 | www.sarkcarriages.co.uk*

DIVING TRIPS
Discover shipwrecks and colourful underwater worlds on a diving trip. Contact: *Andy Leaman | tel. 01481 83 25 65 | www.simplysark.co.uk*

BEACHES

The island's tremendously rugged, steep coastal cliffs provide shelter for many secluded, divinely beautiful bays. You can reach some of the beaches down narrow footpaths – you'll come across the best views of the island as you walk. No cafés or kiosks disturb the tranquillity, so make sure you pack a picnic.

DIXCART BAY ☼ (128 B5) (*M N7*)
A true gem among the bays on the south coast. A path leads to a small waterfall and then down to the beach. You can reach the sands through a gate in the rock. A fairy-tale carpet of wild bluebells covers *Dixcart valley* in the spring. The valley itself leads into the bay below. From the enchanting valley there are also steep paths leading to neighbouring *Derrible Bay* where you can swim at low tide.

EPERQUERIE LANDING
(128 B4) (*M M5*)
Remote, small swimming beach (at low tide) in less frequented north-eastern Sark.

LA GRANDE GRÈVE ☼
(128 B5) (*M M7*)
The most spectacular beach on the island! Plenty of steps lead down from La Coupée which makes it very isolated.

LITTLE SARK'S BEACHES
(128 B5–6) (*M M7*)
Footpaths lead from the Sablonnerie garden restaurant in the centre of Little Sark to the exquisite *Venus Pool,* an attractive rock pool in the south that's great for bathing at low tide. Loop trails lead to the coastal cliffs of *Port Gorey.* As you walk, you'll pass the island's short-lived 19th-century silver mine.

ENTERTAINMENT

The *Mermaid Tavern (junction of Rue Lucas)* is a popular watering hole. *Island Hall* is an island hub that stages concerts and performances.

HERM & SARK

WHERE TO STAY

LA MARGUERITE (128 B5) *(N6)*
A centrally located Miss Marple-style cottage. A friendly family business. *3 rooms | Rue Hotton | tel. 01481 83 22 66 | www.sercq.com | Budget*

LA SABLONNERIE ⭐ (128 B5) *(M7)*
Frequently called one of Great Britain's best country house hotels, this ensemble of old cottages (some 400 years old) is a place of real peace. With no TV to spoilt the tranquillity, you can relax in the beautiful garden or have an excellent dinner beside the fire. The hotel has a pretty tea garden, and the restaurant is famous for its lobster. *22 rooms | Little Sark | tel. 01481 83 20 61 | www.sablonneriesark.com | Moderate*

STOCKS HOTEL (128 B5) *(N6)*
Luxury country living in this family hotel located in Sark's blossoming centre. The pampering doesn't stop when you sit down to eat. *20 rooms | Le Manoir Valley | tel. 01481 83 20 01 | www.stockshotel.com | Expensive*

SUE'S B & B AND TEA GARDEN (128 B4) *(M–N6)*
The owners are descendants of the first settlers 450 years ago and have plenty to relate. The tea garden is idyllic and guests feel at home. Centrally located next to the old mill. *4 rooms | Cae de Mat | tel. 01481 83 21 07 | www.suebnb.com | Budget*

Birdwatching by boat: on the move with George Guille off Sark

LE VIEUX CLOS (128 B5) *(M–N6)*
A small guesthouse with pleasant rooms. *6 rooms | Rue du Moulin | tel. 01481 83 23 41 | www.levieuxclos.co.uk | Budget*

INFORMATION

VISITOR CENTRE (128 B4–5) *(N6)*
The Avenue | tel. 01481 83 23 45 | www.sark.co.uk

DISCOVERY TOURS

① THE CHANNEL ISLANDS AT A GLANCE

START: ① Somerville Hotel
END: ㉗ St Peter Port

6 days
actual bus journey approx. 4 hours

Distance:
➡ almost 280 km/174 mi

COSTS: approx. £800–1,350/person (overnight stays, meals, admissions, bike hire, bus, ferry)
WHAT TO PACK: binoculars

IMPORTANT TIPS: On day one adapt your programme to the tidal times to reach all destinations.

British island-hopping par excellence off northern France! Travel at a leisurely pace with plenty of activities on the way: go exploring for a week from Jersey

You can find these tours as an app at: go.marco-polo.com/cis

Would you like to explore the places that are unique to this region? Then the Discovery Tours are just the thing for you – they include terrific tips for stops worth making, breathtaking places to visit, selected restaurants and fun activities. It's even easier with the Touring App: download the tour with map and route to your smartphone using the QR Code on pages 2/3 or from the website address in the footer below – and you'll never get lost again even when you're offline.

TOURING APP

→ p. 2/3

to Guernsey and Sark, and experience three unique island worlds with rocky coastlines, subtropical plants and dramatic beaches.

When you have checked in at the ❶ **Somerville Hotel** → p. 51 **in St Aubin** an ideal walk – at low tide! – is the 500-m/1,640-ft causeway over the seabed to ❷ **St Aubin's Fort** → p. 48. Coastal forts across the seabed are one of Jersey's highlights! **Carry on along the small street in the harbour to the start of the Railway Walk**, which continues with no traffic for one-and-a-half hours to

DAY 1
❶ Somerville Hotel
1 km/0.6 mi
❷ St. Aubin's Fort
8 km/5 mi

Photo: Mont Orgueil Castle

99

Guernsey
(Guernesey)

Channel Islands (GB)
Îles Anglo-Normandes (GB)

Jersey

---

③ Corbière Lighthouse

7 km/4.4 mi

④ St Ouen's Bay

4 km/2.5 mi

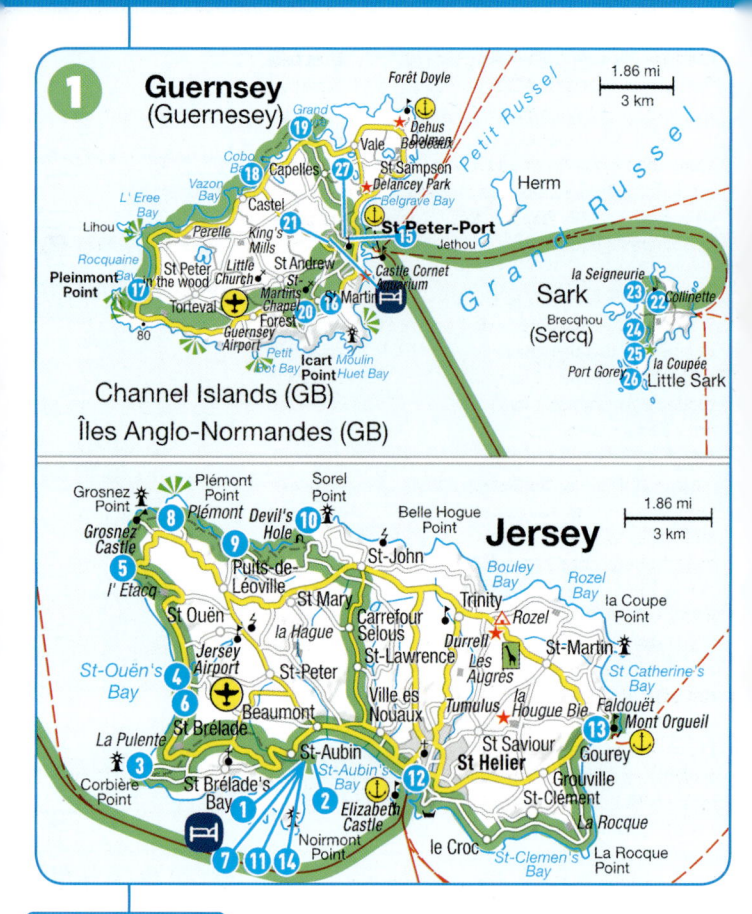

③ **Corbière Lighthouse → p. 34**, which is also only accessible on foot at low tide. Then, it's time for coffee in the restaurant **Corbière Phare** with a fantastic view of the lighthouse and the tower once built by the German army.

From the bus stop near the restaurant, you now take Bus No. 22 (hourly) and alight at the Watersplash bar and restaurant in the heart of ④ St Ouen's Bay → p. 37, Jersey's expansive and sandy western side for surfers and sand yachts. You can hire a body board here at the surf school or simply enjoy a stroll along the beach. Pure relaxation is the name of the game in one of the cool beach

100   You can find these tours as an app at: go.marco-polo.com/cis

DISCOVERY TOURS

cafés like **Big Vern's**. Had enough of chillaxing? **Then take the same bus route to L'Étacq** to sample a few fresh oysters at the funky fish shack ❺ **Faulkner Fisheries → p. 36**. You can spend the evening in one of the beach restaurants **along the Grande Route des Mielles** and watch the surfers dancing in the sunset. Things are really relaxed e.g. in ❻ **El Tico → p. 36**. **Take Bus Nos. 22 and 12 back to the** ❼ **Somerville Hotel**.

Put on sturdy footwear to enjoy a day out hiking! **Take Bus No. 22 again to L'Étacq. Walk across the coastal road as far as the hairpin bend to the signposted coastal path that starts here** and that you follow during the day. It continues for one and a half hours around the north-eastern coastal plateau to the narrow inlet at ❽ **Plémont Bay → p. 42**: a jewel with a bathing beach – at low tide – a cave and café for the first stop. During the next one or two hours, carry on hiking and enjoy the fabulous views and places to stop until you reach **the next bay, Grève de Lecq**. Here, head **200 m/656 ft inland** for a generous lunch at the very rustic pub ❾ **Le Moulin de Lecq** *(daily | tel. 01534 48 28 18 | Budget–Expensive)*! **Later, return to the bay and head for the cliff path. For the next one and a half hours continue in an easterly direction on the cliff path.** In the afternoon, you arrive at the ❿ **Devil's Hole → p. 39** and the nearby country guesthouse **Priory Inn**. You can stay in this pub-restaurant until dinner is served from 6pm (a fabulous seafood platter!) and then return **with Bus No. 7 via St Helier** back to St Aubin and the ⓫ **Somerville Hotel**.

Today, **at the Old War Tunnel at the start of the Railway Walk in St Aubin** you can hire bikes *(www.littletrain.co.uk)* and explore the flatter areas of the south and east coast, which are most affected by the low tides. **On the promenade** you can avoid the traffic and about half an hour later you arrive in the capital ⓬ **St Helier → p. 51**. Cycle **along the harbour area** to the large sea pool at **Havre des Pas → p. 114** – it's safe to go swimming here. **On the next jetty heading eastwards** you can enjoy a break outdoors at the cult **Thai Dicq Shack**. Then, you cycle around Jersey's south-eastern point. **In Gorey**, you will find the majestic castle ⓭ **Mont Orgueil Castle → p. 44**. The castle is well worth a visit – it has the most breathtaking view of Jersey! **The route back to** ⓮ **Somerville Hotel is then 18 km/11.2 mi.**

---

❺ Faulkner Fisheries

5 km/3.1 mi

❻ El Tico

8 km/5 mi

❼ Somerville Hotel

DAY 2

18 km/11.2 mi

❽ Plémont Bay

4 km/2.5 mi

❾ Le Moulin de Lecq

5 km/3.1 mi

❿ Devil's Hole

17 km/10.6 mi

⓫ Somerville Hotel

DAY 3

6 km/3.7 mi

⓬ St Helier

13 km/8.1 mi

⓭ Mont Orgueil Castle

18 km/11.2 mi

⓮ Somerville Hotel

101

DAY 4

57 km/35.4 mi

⑮ St Peter Port

DAY 5

6 km/3.7 mi

⑯ Sausmarez Manor

10 km/6.2 mi

⑰ Fort Grey

9 km/5.6 mi

⑱ Cobo Bay

3 km/1.9 mi

⑲ Grand Havre

32 km/19.9 mi

⑳ The Captain's

6 km/3.7 mi

㉑ St Peter Port

DAY 6

19 km/11.8 mi

㉒ La Seigneurie

1 km/0.6 mi

㉓ Window in the Rock

3 km/1.9 mi

Change islands by ferry *(www.condorferries.co.uk)* and with your luggage: **from St Helier you travel by boat to Guernsey's enchanting mini-metropolis ⑮ St Peter Port → p. 72**. You should definitely visit Victor Hugo's fascinating poet's residence **Hauteville House**, if there is still time after the ferry's arrival. After a stroll through the steeply situated town you can enjoy a meal on the terrace at the **Terrace Garden** and admire the view over the forest of masts in the harbour. The hotel **Les Rocquettes** has a large indoor pool.

An island round tour by bus from St Peter Port only takes about one hour and a half. **Bus No. 91 travels hourly all along the coast.** It's only a stone's throw to the country house of the former island head ⑯ **Sausmarez Manor → p. 62**. Take a walk here through INSIDER TIP **a subtropical maze** filled with numerous picturesque sculptures! **The next stop is Pleinmont in the south west.** Enjoy a short walk along the west coast to the whitewashed round tower of the shipwreck museum ⑰ **Fort Grey → p. 65**. Directly opposite, an intact shipwreck has been exhibited since 2016. **Then, carry on to ⑱ Cobo Bay → p. 68**. Here, you can enjoy a fantastic swim and at high tide the water laps at the sea wall. After your swim you can dine at the **Cobo Bay Hotel** and watch the Ferraris or Porsches that occasionally drive past.

Take a while longer to explore the green area around the bay ⑲ **Grand Havre → p. 71** with the characteristic Martello **Rousse Tower → p. 70**. **Travel back on the next bus to St Peter Port and take Bus No. 81:** this takes you to the enchanting south-east, **where you can get out at the country hotel Bella Luce. Only two minutes across the road La Fausse de Haut,** you will find your restaurant for the evening, ⑳ **The Captain's → p. 64**. You can chat to many locals over a beer and excellent fish dishes. **The last bus back to ㉑ St Peter Port and your hotel is 8.32pm!**

From the pier of the Sark Shipping Company *(www.sarkshippingcompany.com)* **in St Peter you can stop off on Sark where cars are banned.** Walk **from the harbour uphill to the island plateau. At the top, head right** to the former residence of the island Seigneur ㉒ **La Seigneurie → p. 94**. Stroll for a while through the open gardens and admire the beautiful pigeon tower. **Back on the dusty road, turn left and left again** and a few minutes later at the ㉓ **Window in the Rock → p. 94** you can look out to sea

DISCOVERY TOURS

to the island of Brecqhou. To reach Little Sark, you can hire a horse-drawn carriage that takes you **over the dizzying land bridge** ㉔ **La Coupée → p. 93**. At the fabulous garden restaurant ㉕ **La Sablonnerie → p. 97** there is time for an extended lunch – the lobster here is famous.

A short walk afterwards to the **southern point** takes quarter of an hour. If you need to freshen up then take a dip in the famous rock pool ㉖ **Venus Pool** – although you can only do so at low tide. **The way back to the harbour is about 4 km/2.5 mi, and from here you return to Guernsey and the hotel in** ㉗ **St Peter Port**.

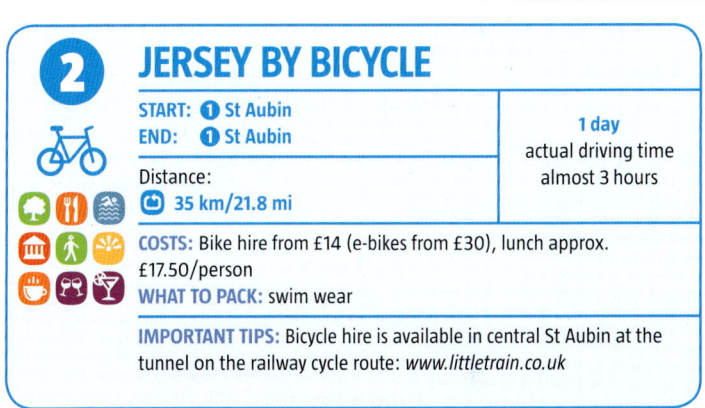

- ㉔ La Coupée
- 1 km/0.6 mi
- ㉕ La Sablonnerie
- 1 km/0.6 mi
- ㉖ Venus Pool
- 21 km/13.1 mi
- ㉗ St Peter Port

2 JERSEY BY BICYCLE

START: ① St Aubin
END: ① St Aubin

Distance: 35 km/21.8 mi

1 day actual driving time almost 3 hours

COSTS: Bike hire from £14 (e-bikes from £30), lunch approx. £17.50/person
WHAT TO PACK: swim wear

IMPORTANT TIPS: Bicycle hire is available in central St Aubin at the tunnel on the railway cycle route: *www.littletrain.co.uk*

Jersey is a paradise for cyclists – although there are many ascents and descents. On green lanes with no cars and on minor roads you can explore Jersey by bike and see much more than car drivers. Signposts are extremely helpful on the labyrinthine routes inland.

09:30am In ① **St Aubin set off in an easterly direction, following the cycle route along the fabulous beach promenade, until after about 3 km/1.9 mi you turn off into the countryside on Cycle Route No. 2.** The scenery changes dramatically: suddenly, you are cycling through forest and following the meandering mill road that gently winds and climbs its way across ② **Waterworks Valley → p. 47**. **At the signposted crossroads on Cycle Route No. 3, take the left turn and shortly afterwards you arrive at the** ③ **Hamptonne Country Life Museum → p. 47**. This is obviously the rural heartland of Jersey. You can spend an hour here at the **café**.

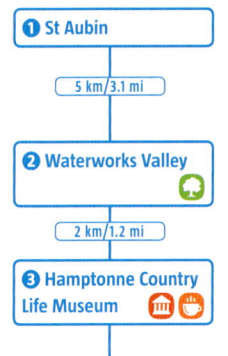

- ① St Aubin
- 5 km/3.1 mi
- ② Waterworks Valley
- 2 km/1.2 mi
- ③ Hamptonne Country Life Museum

103

- 8 km/5 mi
- **4 Priory Inn**
- 1 km/0.6 mi
- **5 Devil's Hole**
- 1 km/0.6 mi
- **6 La Mare Wine Estate**
- 3 km/1.9 mi
- **7 Grève de Lecq**
- 9 km/5.6 mi
- **8 St Ouen's Bay**
- 7 km/4.4 mi
- **1 St Aubin**

12:00pm Continue for a while longer on Route 3 in a westerly direction and at the crossroads head northwards on Route 4. In the locality of St John you reach the first main road and a village. **At the church, turn off onto Route 1 in a westerly direction** and now head for Jersey's northern high plateau. Soon, you will reach the steep north coast for the first time. The **4 Priory Inn** *(daily | La Grande Rue | tel. 01534 48 53 07 | Moderate)* makes an inviting lunch venue in the beer garden. Afterwards, enjoy a short walk to the rocky coast at the **5 Devil's Hole → p. 39**.

Back on the bike, only two or three minutes later you have another reason to get off again: for a wine tasting and digestive schnapps at **6 La Mare Wine Estate → p. 40**. Route No. 1 now takes you in a westerly direction. Suddenly, far below is **7 Grève de Lecq → p. 41**, where you can cool off in the sea.

03:30pm You can only leave the dream bay via a very steep road. Route 1 takes you, after the turn-off to Les Landes, to the west coast. Beforehand, enjoy the **INSIDER TIP** wonderful view along the 7 km/4.4 mi coastal route that lies ahead of you. **On arrival down in 8 St Ouen's Bay → p. 37, you leave Route No. 1 and simply head along the breathtaking surfers' coast.** Stop for a swim and some light refreshments at one of the beach bars! Late in the afternoon, **finally cycle via the Railway Walk (Route 1) and gently downhill back to 1 St Aubin**.

The tour starts and ends at the pretty harbour of St Aubin

104 You can find these tours as an app at: go.marco-polo.com/cis

DISCOVERY TOURS

③ ON FOOT ALONG JERSEY'S NORTH COAST

START: ① Bonne Nuit Bay
END: ⑥ Rozel Bay

Distance:
➡ ca. 12 km/7.5 mi

1 day
actual walking time
almost 4 hours

COSTS: lunch and dinner approx. £25–35/person
WHAT TO PACK: swim wear, binoculars, depending on weather rainwear or sun screen

IMPORTANT TIPS: the starting point and end connect with the scheduled bus service. Bus timetable: *www.libertybus.je*

Jersey offers plenty of wonderful hiking opportunities. The most breathtaking highlights are along the impressive rocky coast in the north. The route has plenty of ascents and descents, sometimes steep. It also has spectacular views over the small bays.

105

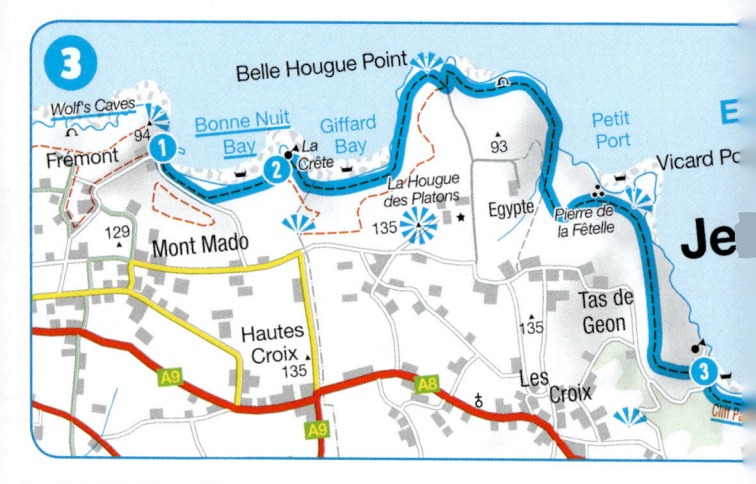

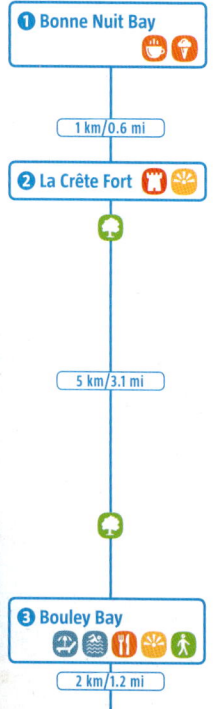

① Bonne Nuit Bay

1 km / 0.6 mi

② La Crête Fort

5 km / 3.1 mi

③ Bouley Bay

2 km / 1.2 mi

11:00am Before setting off in ① **Bonne Nuit Bay → p. 41** enjoy some an ice cream or coffee from the snack bar. **Then, follow the road above the bay, turning left onto the coast path and soon you will notice the signposts for the high route or low route. Take the low route and stop soon afterwards** at the comfortably furnished small coastal fort ② **La Crête Fort**, which Jersey Heritage has converted into self-catering accommodation.

There is a fabulous view in both directions over the bay. Then, walk along the narrow footpath through the ferns blowing gently in the wind. The steep sections have good steps. Usually, only a few hikers are on this stretch of the path, so there ought to be few disruptions to the romantic setting of a INSIDERTIP **small, rocky turret** about half way to Bouley Bay.

01:00pm After three quarters of the almost 6-km/ 3.7-mi section as far as Bouley Bay, **descend through a woodland and the sea is not far away.** Then, carry on uphill through the beautiful woodland, and you reach another plateau where you suddenly look down onto ③ **Bouley Bay → p. 41**. The eagle-eye view over the coastal shrubbery to the rolling bay is absolutely fabulous. Now, it's time for a long and relaxing break: for a walk along the beach, a swim and lunch at the café **Mad Mary**, a premise which serves excellent burgers.

You can find these tours as an app at: go.marco-polo.com/cis

DISCOVERY TOURS

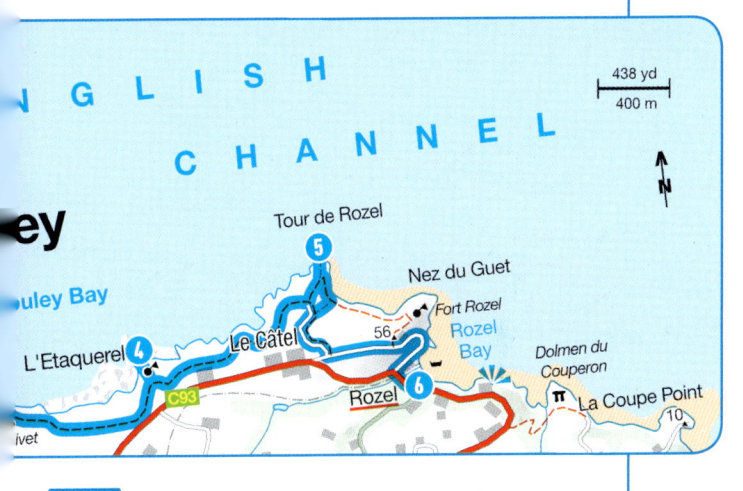

04:30pm Continue in an easterly direction. From the hotel, take the coast path again and follow the signposts out of the bay, until you can admire the wonderful views high above the bay and along the rocky coast as far as France. On the way, you pass a short path to the ruins of the 18-century ❹ **L'Etacquerel Fort**. About 3 km/1.9 mi after Bouley Bay you head across carpets of ferns and through the gnarled coastal woodland to reach the rocky plateau ❺ **White Rock**. The path leads to an isolated country road Rue du Câtel that heads down to the charming coastal village **Rozel** on ❻ **Rozel Bay** → p. 42. A stroll by brightly painted cottages, almost in northern style, leads you to the high harbour defence wall where, 20 m/65.6 ft below, boats with long sails are anchored with chains. You can dine and enjoy a drink in the pleasant Rozel Pub – and the bus stops outside the door.

❹ L'Etacquerel Fort

| 2 km/1.2 mi |

❺ White Rock

| 2 km/1.2 mi |

❻ Rozel Bay

At the colourful beach cottages in Rozel Bay, you are at the end of the tour

4 COASTAL WALK NEAR ST PETER PORT

START: ① South Esplanade
END: ⑦ Fermain Bay

3–4 hours actual walking time approx. 1 hour

Distance: ➡ a good 4 km/2.5 mi
difficulty: very easy

COSTS: lunch approx. £13/person
WHAT TO PACK: swim wear, sturdy shoes

IMPORTANT TIPS: back by bus (Nos. 12, 91, 93). Bus timetable: *www.buses.gg*

This easygoing coastal walk starting at St Peter Port allows you to discover the richness of Guernsey's coast in the smallest spaces: relics of various coastal fortifications, bathing facilities with and without beach as well as a (flower) forest and a gourmet café.

① South Esplanade
  1.7 km/1 mi
② La Valette Underground Military Museum
  400 m/1,312 ft
③ La Valette Bathing Pools
  200 m/656 ft
④ Clarence Battery
  1 km/0.6 mi

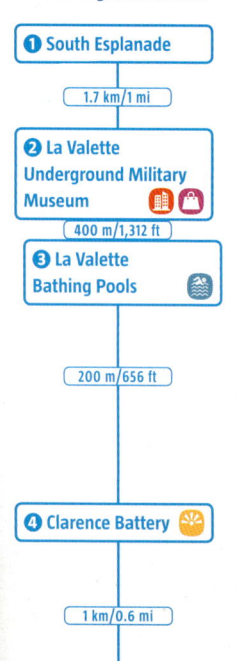

10:00am From the ① **South Esplanade** head southwards along the coast road. You will travel through two former German army tunnels along the old German road project to Fermain Bay: you should look round the quirky shop of the current ② **La Valette Underground Military Museum → p. 76**. Another unusual attraction situated between the bunkers are the tidal pools ③ **INSIDER TIP La Valette Bathing Pools**; despite their imposing concrete design worn away by the high tides, the rock pools invite you to jump in.

You can walk past the next bunkers with the **aquarium,** but don't miss the museum-like and military style plateau with its canons, built in 1782, to defend against Napoleon – ④ **Clarence Battery behind the aquarium:** there is a magnificent view as far as Herm! In a short distance, you have already walked past a wide variety of coastal defences.

108 You can find these tours as an app at: go.marco-polo.com/cis

DISCOVERY TOURS

11:30am Shortly afterwards, **on a level with the wonderful view of Soldier's Bay,** a granite stone wall along a steep woodland is reminiscent of Fort George, which replaced Castle Cornet as a garrison fort and was used by the German army as a radar station. It was bombed by the British and is now an expensive residential quarter. The nearby woodland is called ❺ **Bluebell Wood → p. 73,** because in May a profusion of bluebells is in flower here.

Stroll a little further along the road **Corniche with its modern villas,** and it feels like an exclusive villa quarter, like in the south of France. Soon afterwards, you are enticed for another swim: **make your descent over the imposing staircase** ❻ **Ozanne Steps to a swimming bay that was once private.**

00:30pm Now, it's just another 300 m/ 984 ft until you arrive at the wonderful ❼ **Fermain Bay → p. 64.** The wet sand is exposed at low tide along with one of Guernsey's 15 fortress towers. The almost Mediterranean atmosphere in the bay and lunch at the first-class **Beach Café → p. 63** make a perfect finish to this walk.

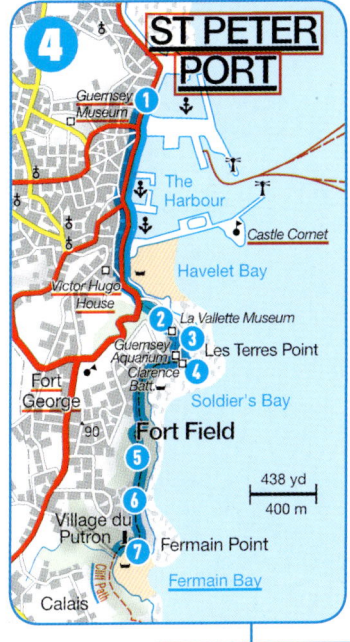

❺ Bluebell Wood
400 m/1,312 ft
❻ Ozanne Steps
400 m/1,312 ft
❼ Fermain Bay

Bluebells, a hyacinth variety, grow profusely in Bluebell Wood

109

SPORTS & ACTIVITIES

Action is in the air: the Channel Islands' mild climate inspires its visitors to take active holidays.

Both of the major Channel Islands, Jersey and Guernsey, are particularly well suited to combining a summery seaside holiday in the shallow, surprisingly quick-warming bays with more active hiking trips. The islands are fabulous cycling terrain with several steep sections, especially in the north of Jersey. Guided kayak tours and stand-up-paddling are also fantastic experiences when the tidal conditions are good. It is similar for coasteering. Several beach yoga sessions provide wellness, also available in the hotels. www.mindfulguernsey.com, www.hoteldefrancejersey.co.uk

ADVENTURE SPORTS

Jersey Adventures (tel. 07797 72 75 03 | www.jerseyadventures.com) offer abseiling (from German military towers), caving, 🟠 coasteering (climbing steep coastal cliffs and diving back down), sand yachting, 🟠 sea kayaking, stand-up paddling … The equivalent on Guernsey is *Outdoor Guernsey (tel. 07781 13 04 03 | www.outdoorguernsey.gg)*, while *Adventure Sark (tel. 01481 83 23 56 | www.adventuresark.com)* offers coasteering and kayaking on Sark.

CYCLING

There's no better way to get to get to know the islands at a comfortable

Photo: A boat in Guernsey's Moulin Huet Bay

The islands' compactness means that outdoor activities are easy to access, so let nature take centre stage!

pace than by bike. Rental bikes *(from £12, e-bike from £23/day or from £45, e-bike from £123/week)* – available to hire almost everywhere – are usually in good condition. Of all the Channel islands, Jersey has the largest cycling network, offering a total of 160 km/99 mi of signposted routes. There are steep downhill trails to the bays in the north, however. On the flatter island of Guernsey, you can discover the low-traffic roads of the interior in a more leisurely way. Cars are only allowed to drive at 24 km/h/15 mph on the green lanes and *ruettes tranquilles* of the larger islands – if they're allowed to drive there at all – making bikes the best way to get around. Cyclists are completely untroubled by cars on Sark, and you'll more often have to fight the strong wind than the traffic on Alderney. Jersey and Guernsey offer very good, detailed cycling guides and maps. *www.jersey.com/cycling-in-jersey, www.jerseybikehire.co.uk, www.go-guernsey.gg/bike-rates*

Mountain bikes don't seem entirely out of place on Jersey's hills

FISHING

Jersey especially offers dramatic spots for coastal fishing: in a clockwise direction at Sorel Point, White Rock, St Catherine's Breakwater, Royal Bay of Grouville, Noirmont Point, Corbière Lighthouse and L'Étacq as well as virtually all the northern bays. More information on sea fishing: *www.fishingjersey.co.uk, www.fishing-guernsey.co.uk*

GOLF

Compared with the size of the area, there are excellent golf facilities on the islands. Jersey boasts eight, Guernsey three and Alderney one golf course. It's standard to play 18 holes. The west coast courses offer charming scenery at Les Mielles and La Moye on Jersey, L'Ancresse on Guernsey and the course on Alderney. *short.travel/kai27*

HIKING

Hikers have the right of way on green lanes and on the magnificent coastal paths everywhere on the islands. If you're looking for something particularly special, the most attractive area for hikers on Guernsey is the coastal region in the south. The entire north coast of Jersey also offers first-class views and exciting descents into small bays. Hiking can be especially enjoyable from March through May, when the coasts and capes explode with floral colour. Take a field guide in your backpack and a small pair of binoculars, they are handy on coastal walks – you can watch seabirds breeding and hunting from May to July. Jersey and Guernsey have released good walking guides with detailed route plans. They can be bought in the Tourist Information centres in St Helier and St Peter Port. Guided tours with thrilling themes from Jersey's National Trust *(www.nationaltrust.je/events)*. A special treat is a two-and-a-half-hour coastal hike along the beach *(£5)* with the nature guy Kazz Padidar *(tel. 07797 88 62 42 | www.wildadventuresjersey.com/bushcraft.html)* in Jersey's St Ouen's Bay. The bushcraft expert will let you instantly sample wild plants while foraging along the shoreline. For more information on hiking: *short.travel/kai5, www.visitguernsey.com/tasty-walks*, for professional guided tours along the shoreline *www.jerseywalkadventures.co.uk* and *www.seajersey.com*

SPORTS & ACTIVITIES

HORSE RIDING

Riders are part of the landscape on Jersey and Guernsey. Why not take a leisurely trot on the green lanes and *ruettes tranquilles* in the interior of the islands? Only experienced riders are allowed to gallop along the beaches, and they can only take to the sand before 10.30am and after 6pm from May to September. Recommended rides are on offer by: *Le Claire Riding & Livery School (Sunnydale | La Rue Militaire | St John | Jersey | tel. 01534 86 28 23); Manor Stables (Rue des Camps | St Martin | Guernsey | tel. 01481 23 82 75). www.jerseyridingclub.co.uk, www.visitguernsey.com/horse-riding*

WATER SPORTS

Sailors can charter boats and hire guides for tours everywhere on the islands. Wind surfers adore the large bays on Jersey and their northern and western counterparts on Guernsey. Alderney also experiences good winds. If you enjoy kayaking, you'll also have fun on all islands. **INSIDER TIP BloKarting offers you top speed! Carting with a sail** in St Ouen's Bay with *Pure Adventure (www.purejersey.com)*. *Seafaris (www.jerseyseafaris.com)* offers dinghy trips and land excursions to island reefs. On Guernsey, there are adrenalin-fuelled rib-dinghy voyages: *www.islandribvoyages.com*

The west coasts of Jersey and Guernsey make excellent destinations for wave riders. Jersey's St Ouen's Bay even attracts surfers from Australia when it's winter Down Under. You can surf year-round in *St Ouen's Bay*, but there's a surf-free period in *St Brelade's Bay, Plémont Bay* and *Grève de Lecq* from 10am to 7pm. Guernsey's *Vazon Bay* is popular, and Alderney's hotspot is *Corblets Bay*. You can hire surfboards and suits, and also learn to surf: *Jersey Surf School | La Grande Route des Mielles | St Ouen's Bay | tel. 07797 71 60 55 | www.jerseysurfschool.co.uk; Guernsey Surf School | Vazon Bay | tel. 07911 71 07 89 | www.guernseysurfschool.co.uk*

Divers swear by the quality of the water and the light on the Channel Islands. Whatever you do, be aware of the strong tides and currents in the waters of the Channel. Jersey's northern bays offer good diving spots near the coast *(Bouley Bay Dive Centre | tel. 01534 86 69 90 | www.scubadivingjersey.com)*. More underwater trips are offered by: *Dive Jersey | 1 Belmont Gardens | St Helier | tel. 01534 88 09 34 | www.divejersey.co.uk; Dive Guernsey | Castle Emplacement | St Peter Port | tel. 01481 71 45 25*

The fashionable sport of stand-up paddling is also becoming popular on the islands. Learn how to paddle standing up on a surfboard for around £25 at Jersey's *Windmadness (St Brelade's Bay | tel. 01534 52 28 88 | www.windmadness.com)*. On Guernsey: *www.guernseysup.com*

Stopover in L'Ancresse Bay on Guernsey

TRAVEL WITH KIDS

The typical Channel Island holidaymaker is over 45 years old, well off, and travels without children. That's because the islands make a pretty pricey destination – especially with kids in tow. But you can also find treasures that money can't buy: car-free islands, unspoilt beaches, extremely clean air, and a perfect island world that is lost in time.

JERSEY

AMAIZIN ADVENTURE PARK
(129 F3) (*m* C11)

An adventure park for the whole family with a range of attractions. A puzzle-filled maize maze, crazy golf, water pistol fighting, tractor driving, a petting zoo, and lots of other attractions. *April–Sept daily 10am–5.30pm | £10.80 (adults and children) | La Hougue Farm | La Grande Route de St Pierre | St Peter | www.jerseyleisure.co.uk*

DURRELL WILDLIFE CONSERVATION TRUST (131 D3) (*m* H11)

An absolute highlight for kids on Jersey! The most exciting sights are the spectacled bear, the orang-utans, and the gorillas. The INSIDER TIP house with both big bat species is especially exciting – it is kept at the right temperature for the vegetarian creatures thanks to a ◯ biomass heating system. *Daily 9.30am–5pm, April–Oct until 6pm | £16, kids up to 16 years, £11.50 | www.durrell.org*

HAVRE DES PAS ● (130 C5) (*m* G14)

Have fun swimming at low tide: this large seawater pool has been in use since the end of the 19th century. There's a shallow kids' section and an area for more serious swimming. You can really let off steam here at the edge of St Helier when the tide's out. It's exciting to see the sea washing back into the pool when the tide changes. *Daily | free entry*

INSIDER TIP TAMBA PARK
(130 B2) (*m* D–E11)

Delightful fun park with big dinosaur sculptures that move on approach, also sculptures carved by Zimbabweans that the entrepreneur Jonathan Ruff brought back to Jersey to support his kitchen for 5,000 African children – target: 20,000. Feed the fish, adventure park and café. *Daily 9am–6pm | £3.95, children £5.95 | La Rue des Varvots | St Lawrence | www.tambaexperience.co.uk*

Crazy golf, a maize maze, a great zoo – and a landscape straight from the pages of Beatrix Potter

DRIFTWOOD CRAFT
(129 F5) (*C13–14*)
Fish 'n' Beads is the name of a sweet little shop on St Brelade's beach where you can transform driftwood and other beach finds into jewellery and accessories. It offers a selection of glass beads and much more that smaller children will love. *By the Wayside Café | sites.google.com/site/fishnbeads*

GUERNSEY

COBO BAY (126 C3) (*D4*)
White sand, pink rocks for climbing and everything you need nearby: a snack bar, fish and chips, a supermarket – a popular family beach at low tide.

OATLANDS VILLAGE (127 E2) (*F3*)
Even the sight of the curious, pointed brick kilns is exciting. Inside, you can have fun learning all about the old craft of kiln-firing bricks and pots. You can watch as they make chocolates, take a visit to the doll's house museum or try your luck at mini golf *(£6.50)*. Kids can have a bounce on the trampolines *(£3)* or romp around in the play barn *(£5.50)*. *Daily 9am–5pm | free entry | Les Gigands | Braye Road | St Sampson | www.oatlands.gg*

INSIDER TIP SAUSMAREZ TRAIN
(127 E5) (*F6*)
A very small train for very small people: your little rascals can travel 500 m/ 1640 ft on the Seigneur of Sausmarez's train through his subtropical garden. *April–Oct daily 10am–4pm | £2; up to 12 years, £1.50 | www.sausmarezmanor.co.uk/trains.html*

ALDERNEY

RIDING (128 A2) (*M2*)
Jill Moore saddles her horses for short rides with kids. *From £25 per hour | Telegraph Track | tel. 07781 42 13 25 | bjmoore65@yahoo.co.uk*

115

FESTIVALS & EVENTS

FESTIVALS & EVENTS

MARCH
A gourmet event at the *Rocquette Cider Company* in Castel: after a walk through the fruit orchards, at the **Rocquette Cider Tour** on Guernsey you can taste nine local ciders and liqueurs, rounded off with home-produced honey and different Guernsey cheese varieties. *www.rocquettecider.com*

MID-APRIL–MID-SEPTEMBER
Herm Island Garden Tours: every Tuesday at 11am, the island manager explains during a two-hour tour how Herm's garden paradise is maintained. *www.herm.com*

MAY
Jersey and Guernsey celebrate **Liberation Day** on 9 May with all kinds of processions and entertainment offers.

MAY–SEPTEMBER
Private **Garden Walks** offer two-hour guided tours through Sark's gardens every Friday. *Tel. 01481 83 23 45*

MID-MAY–MID-JUNE
For the **orchids in bloom** on Guernsey (*Les Vicheries Lane*) and Jersey (*Le Noir Pré*) paths are prepared through ten-thousands of wild orchids.

SECOND HALF OF JUNE
INSIDER TIP *June in Bloom* is Jersey's ultimate garden festival, held in the second half of June. All of Jersey's floral secrets will be revealed on guided tours through the island's private parks, gardens and woods; through the Durrell zoo in the evening; and through the microclimate zones and orchid meadows of the west coast.

JULY
La Fête de Musique à la Ville takes place in the last week of July on Guernsey in St Peter Port with music, street processions and fireworks – Guernsey's carnival!

JULY–SEPTEMBER
On Sundays, the North Esplanade in St Peter Port is closed for traffic and becomes festival space for art, creativity and food: the **Seafront Sundays**. *www.tasteguernsey.com*

MID-JULY–MID-AUGUST
Castle Cornet in St Peter Port opens its doors on four Fridays from mid-July for a great **castle festival** with live music.

AUGUST

Alderney Week in early August is a fun carnival with over 100 events.

On the second weekend in August Sark is packed for the musical ***Sark Summer Festival***. *www.sarksf.com*

The highlight of the year is the ⭐ ***Battle of Flowers*** on Jersey *(www.battleofflowers.com)* and Guernsey *(www.northshowguernsey.org.uk)* for two days in August – parades of floats decorated in flowers roll through the capitals. On Jersey, the INSIDER TIP ***Moonlight Parade*** the next evening is a summer night's dream with illuminated festival floats.

Sark's night sky is one of the darkest skies in Great Britain. Around the 12 August, the festival ***Wish Upon a Star*** brings together stargazers and astronomers for the Perseid Meteor Shower. *www.darkskyisland.net*

MID-SEPTEMBER

International Air Display *(www.jerseyairdisplay.org.uk):* In mid-September in Jersey's St Aubin's Bay one of the biggest air shows in Europe with many vintage aircraft.

A three-day sailing ship event off St Helier is the ***Jersey Regatta*** – it's a competition and festival. *jerseyregatta.com*

OCTOBER

On the second weekend of October, ***La Faîs'sie d'Cidre*** is a celebration of traditional cider production. *short.travel/kai28*

At the ***Tennerfest*** more than 150 restaurants on Jersey and Guernsey offer a full menu for £10–20 until mid-November. *www.tennerfest.com*

Alderney has a counterpart, the three-week ***Fabulous Fifteen Food Festival***. *short.travel/kai25*

PUBLIC HOLIDAYS

1 Jan	New Year
March/April	Good Friday and Easter Monday
1st Mon in May	Labour Day
9 May	Liberation Day
Last Mon in May	Spring Bank Holiday
Last Mon in Aug	Summer Bank Holiday (on Alderney: 1st Mon in Aug)
25 Dec	Christmas Day
26 Dec	Boxing Day

LINKS, BLOGS, APPS & CO.

LINKS & BLOGS

short.travel/kai7 A compendium of cycling on 563 km/350 mi routes on Jersey, including commented touring recommendations and maps to download

www.nationaltrust.gg The website of Guernsey's National Trust – a foundation dedicated to preserving and promoting the island's natural and historical heritage. Find out about events, walks and tours organised by the Trust. Jersey's National Trust is online at http://www.nationaltrust.je

www.jerseytravel.com/blog An up-to-date blog about Jersey. The well-written articles by a number of authors give the lowdown on what's going on, eating recommendations, the "activity of the week", and what it's like to live on the island

visitguernsey.com Lots of information about Guernsey: flowers, occupation period, literatur, events, food …

www.jerseybites.com Current issues on what is serverd in Jersey's restaurants and in which atmosphere. First-hand and very helpful

www.jerseytravel.com A tour operator's website with up-to-date news about reasonably priced accommodation, events and travel-related topics

short.travel/kai29 and short.travel/kai33 Excellent research in the minefield of Jersey's tax haven: the rise and fall of the island's economy

www.facebook.com/outdoorguernsey Sea kayak trips, coasteering and other coastal adventures from outdoor fans on Guernsey

www.jerseyandguernsey.com/blog A useful blog about island holidays

APPS

Jersey Virtual Heritage Pocket Museum Jersey's historic finds in 3-D and augmented reality

Regardless of whether you are still researching your trip or already on the Channel Islands: these addresses will provide you with more information, videos and networks to make your holiday even more enjoyable

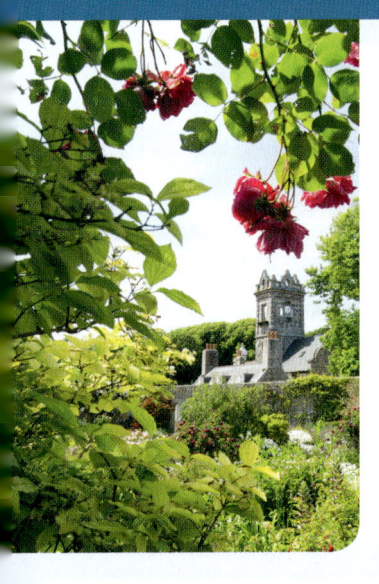

My Tide Times A comprehensive app that gives you a daily and weekly forecast of the tide times for hundreds of coastal destinations in the UK. Tide 7 is a good alternative for Android users. Will help you get to Corbière Lighthouse with dry feet

Walking & Cycling Guernsey So you don't get lost walking or cycling on the *ruettes tranquilles* on Guernsey

Channel News App – A free, award-winning app with all the latest news from the Channel Islands. Keep up to date with exactly what's going on in the archipelago as you hop from island to island

VIDEOS & MUSIC

www.teachingthroughnature.co.uk Between March and October, the active Alderney Wildlife Trust set up webcams on the colonies of puffins and gannets off Alderney

short.travel/kai36 An eleven-minute video about coasteering on Guernsey filmed from the participant perspective

short.travel/kai8 Video about the British "land artist" Andy Goldsworthy. Since 2011, on Alderney near the coast, eleven large balls of pressed earth have been placed that erode over time – meanwhile, the number has sunk to five balls

short.travel/kai30 Six-minute film about the landscapes and coast of Herm

http://vimeo.com/37349918 A beautiful video of 25,000 time-lapse photographs of Guernsey by Kaspars Daleckis. The product of 200 hours' work, it's sure to whet your appetite for this beautiful island

www.youtube.com/user/DURRELLvideos/featured A wealth of videos about Gerald Durrell, the Durrell Wildlife Conservation Trust and the zoo on Jersey. The videos feature some famous names, including David Attenborough, John Cleese, and Stephen Fry. You can also check out their conservation campaign at www.thelonelydodo.com

The Publisher shall not be held responsible for the contents of the links, blogs, apps, etc. listed here

TRAVEL TIPS

ARRIVAL

You can reach the Channel Islands from London within one to two hours. From London City airport you can travel with Blue Islands *(from approx. £30 / blueislands.com)* to Jersey and Guernsey. Flights to Guernsey are also offered from London Gatwick airport by British Airways *(www.britishairways.com)*. Aurigny Air Services *(www.aurigny.com)* also departs from Stansted and Gatwick and flies with 10-seater planes – the baggage allowance is just 15 kg/33 lbs – over Jersey to Guernsey and then onward to Alderney. Blue Islands fly between the islands. easyJet fly from London Southend (www.Easyjet.com) to Jersey. Prices for flights start at around £65 return. From the US, Canada or Australia, you'll have to take a flight to London and switch planes when you arrive. You'll sometime also have to change airports in London, something that takes from 60 to 90 minutes by bus.

Condor Ferries connect the English ports of Poole, Weymouth and Portsmouth with St Malo (France) via Jersey and Guernsey. From St Malo the travel time is about one hour to Jersey and about two hours to Guernsey. The catamaran fast ferries with Condor Ferries depart daily during the main season, less frequently from October to March. For a private car with two people, depending on the season and week day, you can pay about £85 (reasonable), and at peak times about £170.

In summer Manche Iles Express links Granville in Normandy with Jersey on a daily basis, and more sporadically Barneville-Carteret and Diélette with Guernsey and Alderney.

The Isle of Sark Shipping Company travels between Guernsey and Sark many times a day. The crossing takes around 50 minutes. The island of Herm can be reached in around 20 minutes by boat from Guernsey. The Little Ferry Company offers passages from Guernsey to Alderney that take an hour.

RESPONSIBLE TRAVEL

It doesn't take a lot to be environmentally friendly whilst travelling. Don't just think about your carbon footprint whilst flying to and from your holiday destination but also about how you can protect nature and culture abroad. As a tourist it is especially important to respect nature, look out for local products, cycle instead of driving, save water and much more. If you would like to find out more about eco-tourism please visit: *www.ecotourism.org*

CAMPER VANS

There are a great many cars on the Channel Islands, meaning that there just isn't any space for a camper van vacation. A quirky exception on Jersey comes in the form of the **INSIDER TIP** beautifully restored VW camper vans owned by Le Riche *(tel. 01534 86 40 73 / www.jerseycamperhire.com)*, offered in season from £150/day. You can spend the night in them at the campsites Beuvelande, Rozel Camping Park and Bleu Soleil.

From arrival to weather

Your holiday from start to finish: the most important addresses and information for your trip to the Channel Islands

CLIMATE, WHEN TO GO

April/May and mid-September to mid-November are excellent times to travel – you'll have lots of good weather and there won't be too many other tourists. It's also easier to find a room without booking in advance during these times. The high season is from June to August. Many attractions are closed in winter.

CONSULATES & EMBASSIES

US EMBASSY
– *33 Nine Elms Lane | London SW11 7US | tel. 020 74 99 90 00*

AUSTRALIAN EMBASSY
– *Australia House | Strand | London WC2B 4LA | tel. 020 73 79 43 34*

CANADIAN HIGH COMMISSION
– *Canada House | Trafalgar Square | London SW1Y 5BJ | tel. 020 70 04 60 00*

CUSTOMS

The Channel Islands don't belong to the EU, making them a tax-free shopping haven. You can buy tax-free goods on the journeys there and back within certain limits. Check the relevant rules for your home country or for your onward destination.

DRIVING

It's best if you don't try to get around the islands by car – on Jersey and Guernsey in particular there are far too many cars in too little space. Driving isn't actually a very practical way to discover the islands anyway. The speed limit ranges between 24 km/h/15 mph on the green lanes and 64 km/h/40 mph on the main roads. You have to display pay cards in your car before 5pm if you want to park – buy them in advance from shops, car rental stores,

CURRENCY CONVERTER

£	$	$	£
1	1.30	1	0.75
3	3.90	3	2.25
5	6.50	5	3.75
13	16.90	13	9.75
40	52	40	30
75	97.50	75	56.25
120	156	120	90
250	325	250	187.50
500	650	500	375

For current exchange rates see www.xe.com

ferry terminals and from tourist information centres. Yellow lines at the side of the road mean you can't park there at any time.

ELECTRICITY

Mains voltage runs at 240 V. You might require an adapter for charging hairdryers, etc. if you're not coming from the UK.

EMERGENCY

Tel. 9 99 and 112

HEALTH

Non-UK citizens have to pay up front when they visit a doctor – holiday health insurance is therefore advisable. UK citizens have to pay for visits to the dentist and for prescription medication.

IMMIGRATION

If you're already legally in the UK, you won't need to go through customs when you enter the Channel Islands. But it's recommended that you carry your passports anyway, or at least some photo ID, and most airlines demand it. If you're arriving from outside the UK, a passport is required.

INFORMATION

Visit Britain provides extensive information about the Channel Islands – but only on their website: *www.visitbritain.com*

The official websites for the islands are *www.jersey.com, www.visitguernsey.com, www.visitalderney.com, www.sark.co.uk, www.herm.com*. Also check out the websites of the daily newspapers – the Guernsey Press *(www.guernseypress.com)* and the Jersey Evening Post *(www.jerseyeveningpost.com)*.

INTERNET ACCESS & WIFI

Most accommodation is very well connected to the internet. Internet cafés are mainly to be found in St Helier and St Peter Port.

MONEY & CREDIT CARDS

You can use cards to get cash from ATMs. Visa and MasterCard are accepted. The

WEATHER IN GUERNSEY

	Jan	Feb	March	April	May	June	July	Aug	Sept	Oct	Nov	Dec
Daytime temperatures in °C/°F	9/48	8/46	11/52	13/55	16/61	19/66	21/70	21/70	19/66	16/61	12/54	10/50
Nighttime temperatures in °C/°F	5/41	4/39	6/43	7/45	10/50	13/55	15/59	15/59	14/57	11/52	8/46	6/43
Sunshine hours/day	2	3	5	7	8	9	8	8	6	6	3	2
Precipitation days/month	14	11	9	9	9	8	9	10	11	12	12	14
Water temperatures in °C/°F	10	9	9	9	11	13	15	16	16	15	13	11

TRAVEL TIPS

Jersey pound is used on Jersey – Guernsey pounds are in circulation on all the other islands. The currency's value is linked to the British pound, which you can also use on all the islands. Island bank notes cannot be used in Great Britain.

PHONE & MOBILE PHONE

Every call to the islands from abroad must start with the national code *0044*. You then drop the first 0 (zero) at the start of the local island area code. The code to ring the US and Canada is *001*. Calls to Australia require the code *0061*. You can use your mobile/cell phone for short calls abroad, but it's recommended that you buy a British prepaid card if you're going to be making lots of calls outside the UK.

POST

Postcards and letters have to bear the stamps of the island you're sending them from – English stamps aren't valid. You can buy stamps from a dozen island post offices.

PRICE DISCOUNT

The Jersey Heritage Pass offers admission to four of the six top museums and castles for the price of three within one week for £30. On Guernsey the pass is called the Discovery Pass.

PUBLIC TRANSPORT

The public buses on Jersey and Guernsey are an excellent way to get around. On Jersey *(www.libertybus.je)* you can get a hop-on-hop-off pass for £30 per week or £8 a day, a single ticket costs £2.20. On Guernsey the bus company *(www.buses.gg)* offers you the possibility to buy a so-called "puffin pass" with £0.55 debited for each stretch.

BUDGETING

Cream Tea	from £8.80/$11.60 for a pot of tea with scones
Snacks	from around £7/$9.30 for a bag of fish and chips
Wine	around £6.20/$8.10 for a glass of wine
Bus journey	£0.55–2.60/$0.75–2.70 for a single journey
Rental car	from £26.50/$35 for a small car per day
Souvenirs	about £88/$115 for a Guernsey pullover

TIME

The Channel Islands are in the same time zone as the UK. Greenwich Mean Time is five hours ahead of US Eastern Time, and 10 hours behind Australian Eastern Time.

TIPPING

Tipping is not expected in pubs. Five to ten per cent is the usual contribution in restaurants and hotels.

WEIGHTS & MEASURES

1 pound = 454 grams (g)
1 pint = 0.568 litres (l)
1 mile = 1.6 kilometres (km)

ROAD ATLAS

■ The green line indicates the Discovery Tour "The Channel Islands at a glance"
■ The blue line indicates the other Discovery Tours

All tours are also marked on the pull-out map

124 Photo: Marble Bay at the southeastern tip of Guernsey

Exploring the Channel Islands

The map on the back cover shows how the area has been sub-divided

Herm

Guernsey

D
E
F
HANNEL
Baie de la Jaonneuse
Le Plomb
Fort le Marchant
Fort Pembroke
L'Ancresse Bay
Fontenelle Bay
Fort Doyle
1
Star Fort
Pembroke Bay
Beaucette Marina
La Varde Dolmen
L'Ancresse Common
La Fontanelle
Ladies Bay
La Rousse Tower
Baie de Port Grat
Croix Besnard
Le Grand Havre
Les Fouaillages
Le Marais
Clos du Valle
Le Dehus Dolmen
Baie de Pêqueries
Rousse
La Turquie
ST SAMPSON
La Passée
La Grève
VALE
Cocagne
Portinfer Bay
L'Islet
Bordeaux
Port Soif
Vale Parish Church
Maraitaine
2
Bordeaux Harbour
Pleinheaume
Les Martins
Oatlands Village
Saltpans
Vale Castle
Grandes Rocques
Grand Fort
Vingtaine de L' Epine
Guernsey Candles
Les Annevilles
St Sampson
Capelles
Les Gigands
Le Mont Crevelt Tower
VALE
ST SAMPSON
La Tonelle
South Side
Houmets
Le Marais
Spur Point
Weymouth
Saumarez Park
Les Quartiers
Ivy Castle
3
Folk Museum
Le Villocq
Telephone Museum
La Ramée
Bouet
Belle Grève Bay
ST PETER PORT
Poole, Portsmouth
Les Varendes
ST PETER PORT
Beau Sejour Leisure Centre
St Anne (Alderney)
Castel Hospital
Herm
CASTEL
Castel Parish Church
Golf Course
Guernsey Museum
La Chaumière
The Harbour
Dielette, Sark
La Monnaie
Government House
Castle Cornet
4
Bailiff's Cross
Havelet Bay
Camptréhard
ST ANDREW
Ville au Roi
Victor Hugo House
La Vallette Museum
Les Terres Point
Guernsey Aquarium
Clarence Batt.
Soldier's Bay
St Helier (Jersey), St. Malo
Four Cabot
Fort George
Les Huriaux
Fort Field
German Underground Hospital
Les Hubits
St Martin's Parish Church
La Grandmère du Chimquière
Carmel
La Beilleuse
Village du Putron
Sausmarez Manor
Mouilpied
Fermain Point
La Chêne
Fermain Bay
La Villette
5
Calais
ST MARTIN
Cliff Path
Les Pages
La Fosse
Le Vallon
Doyle Column
Cliff Path
Le Petit Port
Martello Tower
Moulin Huet Bay
Petit Bôt Bay
Jerbourg
Icart
Portelet Bay
Saint's Bay
St Martin's Point
Jerbourg Point
6
Icart Point

Alderney / Sark

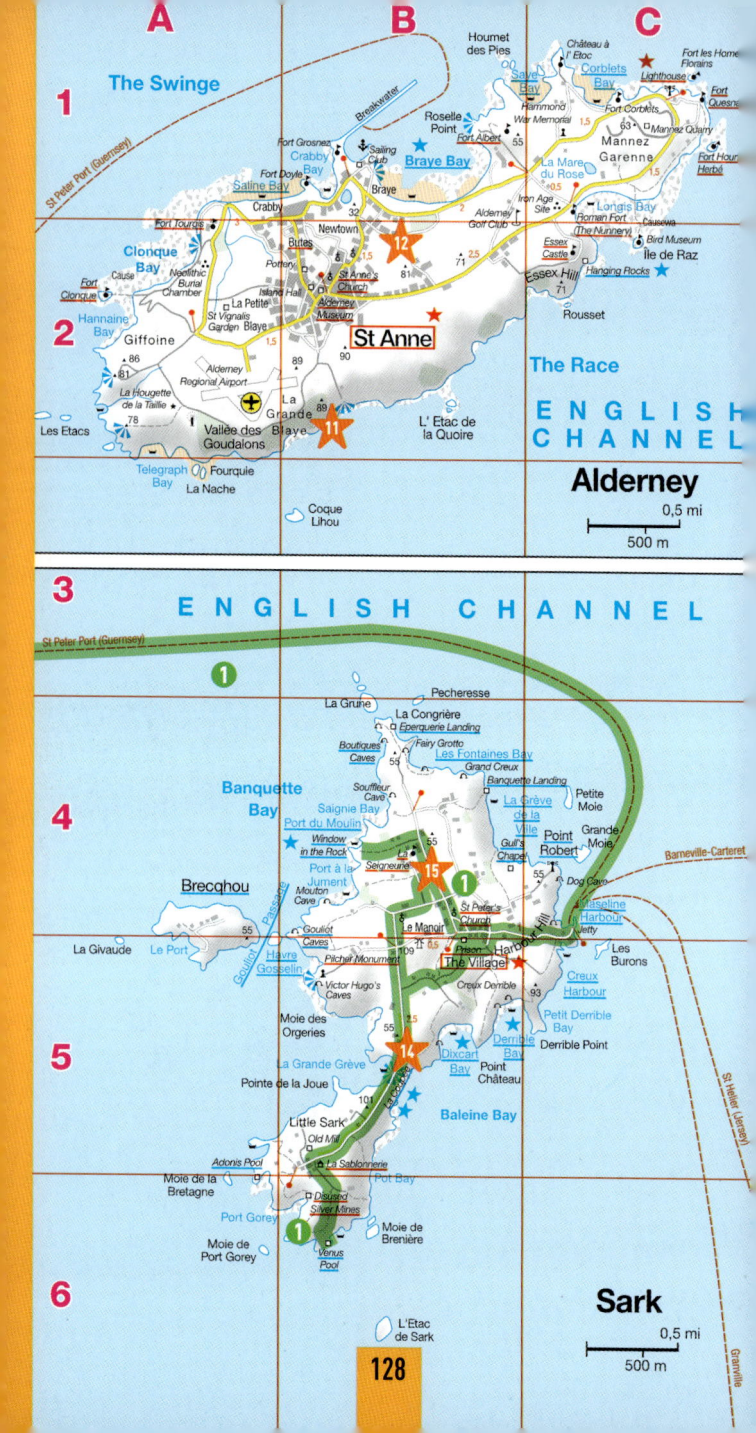

128

D
E
F
1
2
3
4
5
6
Plémont Point
Grosnez Point
Plémont Bay
Grosnez Castle
La Cotte à la Chèvre
Grottes Plémont
Plémont
Grand Becquet
Racecourse
Portinfer
Plémont Candlecraft
Ville la Bas
Rouge Nez
L'Âne
Île Agois
Les Reuses
Grève de Lecq
Dolmen des Geonnais
Le Pinacle
Lecq
Châtel de Lecq
Grève de Lecq Barracks & North Coast Visitor Center
La Houque Mauger
Ville Bagot
ST MARY
Grande Etaquerel
La Villaise
Moulin de Lecq
Les Colombiers
Petite Etaquerel
Battle of Flowers Museum
Shire Horse Farm
Léoville
Treasures of the Earth
L'Etacq
L'Etacq Woodcraft
St Ouen's Village
St Peter's Mill
St Mary Parish Church
La Saline
Jersey Pearl Centre
Dolmen du Mont Grantez
Lewis Tower
Les Laveurs
Channel Islands Military Museum
ST OUEN
Elysée
Ville au Bas
St Ouen's Parish Church
St Ouen's Manor
La Mielle de Morville
La Hougue
St Peter's House
Kempt Tower
a Maizin Maze
St Peter's Village
St Ouen's Pond
Old Fort
La Presse
Les Mielles
Val de la Mare Reservoir
L'Ouisière
The White Menhir
Sunset Nurserie
St Peter's Parish Church
St Ouen's Bay
Les Mielles Golf
ST PETER
Jersey Airport
Le Port
Les Landes
Les Ormes Golf Course
Saut Falluet
Ville de Quennevais
Le Braye
Les Blanches Banques
Belle Vue Pleasure Park
Les Quennevais
ST BRELADE
La Carrière
La Rocco Tower
La Moye Golf Course
St Brelade
Lavender Farm
La Pulente
L'Oeillère
Los Creux Millenium Country Park
Shell Garden
Petit Port
La Sergentée
St Brelade's Parish Church
Mont Sohier
Le Grouet
La Moye
Fishermen's Chapel
Corbière Point
Table des Marthes
Corbière
Les Creux
Corbière Lighthouse
Bouilly Port
St Brelades's Bay
Mont Fiquet
La Rosière
Beauport Bay
Ouaisné Bay
Ouaisné
Fiquet Bay
La Cotte Point
La Cotte de St Brelade
La Fosse
Point la Moye
Point le Fret
Portelet Bay
B34
B65
B55
B35
B64
B53
B40
A12
B69
B32
B26
B41
B36
B42
B43
B25
A13
B44
B66
B83
B57
Jersey
0,5 mi
500 m

130

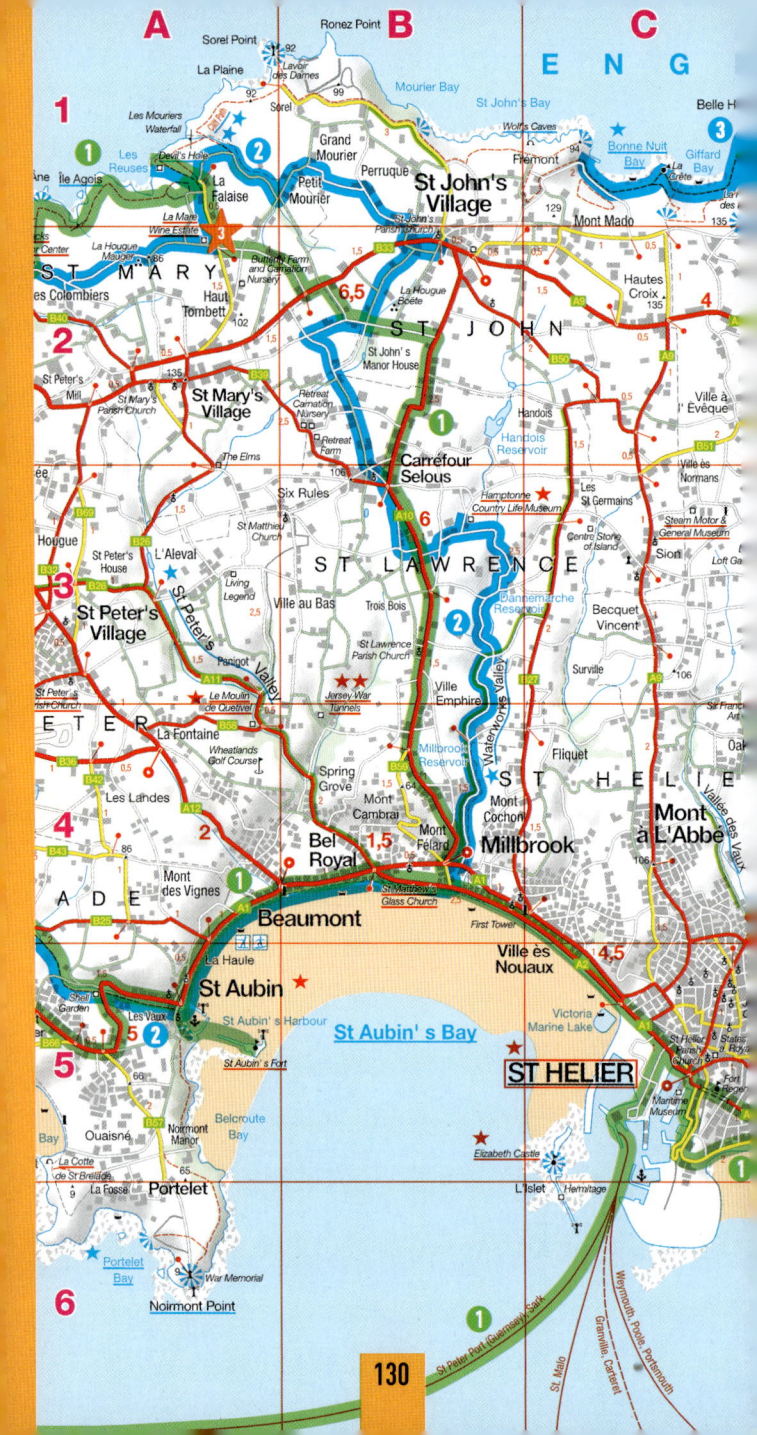

D
E
F
SH CHANNEL
Jersey
0,5 mi
500 m
1
2
3
4
5
6
Petit Port
Vicard Point
Pierre de la Fételle
Tas de Geon
135
Bouley Bay
Tour de Rozel
Nez du Guet
Fort Rozel
Rozel Bay
L'Etaquerel
Le Câtel
56
Cliff Path
Jardin d' Olivet
Trinity Parish Church
Le Puits
Rozel
La Fosse
Dolmen du Couperon
La Coupe Point
10
Les Augrès Manor
Ville Brée
Ville ès Nouaux
Fliquet
Fliquet Bay
Les Câteaux Earthwork
Durrell Wildlife Conservation Trust
Rozel Manor
St Catherine's
63
Verclut Point
TRINITY
ST MARTIN
St Catherine's Breakwater
Belval
89
Maufant Manor
Croix au Maître
St Martin's Parish Church
Martello Tower
St Catherine's Bay
Eric Young Orchid Foundation
La Perelle
77
Victoria Village (La Boucterie)
Ville ès Gaudins
Augrès
Beau Vallon
Archirondel Tower
Hâvre de Fer
Archirondel
La Crête Point
Grands Vaux Reservoir
ST SAVIOUR
Maufant
62
Anne Port
Carrefour au Clercq
Faldouët
Dolmen de Faldouët
Grand
Five Oaks
Agriculture History and Railway Museum
La Hougue Bie
Ville ès Philippes
Gorey
Jersey Pottery
Gorey Harbour
Mont Orgueil Castle (Gorey Castle)
St Saviour's Parish Church
Queens Valley Reservoir
Gorey Village
Fort William
Carteret, Diélette
Photographic Museum
Beau Désert
77
Moulin de Bas
Le Boulivot
Ville ès Renauds
Royal Jersey Golf Course
Beauvoir
Maison du Haut
GROUVILLE
Le Bourg
Fort Henry
Royal Bay of Grouville
Longueville Manor Hotel
Radier
Grouville Parish Church
Bagot
Trading Estate
Grouville Arsenal
Grouville
Fauvic
Verclut
St Clément's Parish Church
Samarès Manor
Dolmen du Mont Ubé
Le Hurel
64
Le Aquez
ST CLEMENT
Le Bourg
Le Haguais
Le Hocq
Pontac
La Rocque Point
Seymour Tower
La Mare
Samares
St Clement's Bay
Platte Rocque Point
Le Nez Point
La Motte (Green Island)
A3
A4
A5
A6
A7
A8
B28
B30
B31
B37
B38
B46
B48
B62
C93

KEY TO ROAD ATLAS

Autobahn · Gebührenpflichtige Anschlussstelle · Gebührenstelle · Anschlussstelle mit Nummer · Rasthaus mit Übernachtung · Raststätte · Kleinraststätte · Tankstelle · Parkplatz mit und ohne WC	Motorway · Toll junction · Toll station · Junction with number · Motel · Restaurant · Snackbar · Filling-station · Parking place with and without WC
Autobahn in Bau und geplant mit Datum der voraussichtlichen Verkehrsübergabe	Motorway under construction and projected with expected date of opening
Zweibahnige Straße (4-spurig)	Dual carriageway (4 lanes)
Fernverkehrsstraße	Trunk road
Straßennummern	Road numbers
Wichtige Hauptstraße	Important main road
Hauptstraße · Tunnel · Brücke	Main road · Tunnel · Bridge
Nebenstraßen	Minor roads
Fahrweg · Fußweg	Track · Footpath
Wanderweg (Auswahl)	Tourist footpath (selection)
Eisenbahn mit Fernverkehr	Main line railway
Zahnradbahn, Standseilbahn	Rack-railway, funicular
Kabinenschwebebahn · Sessellift	Aerial cableway · Chair-lift
Autofähre · Personenfähre	Car ferry · Passenger ferry
Schifffahrtslinie	Shipping route
Naturschutzgebiet · Sperrgebiet	Nature reserve · Prohibited area
Nationalpark · Naturpark · Wald	National park · natural park · Forest
Straße für Kfz. gesperrt	Road closed to motor vehicles
Straße mit Gebühr	Toll road
Straße mit Wintersperre	Road closed in winter
Straße für Wohnanhänger gesperrt bzw. nicht empfehlenswert	Road closed or not recommended for caravans
Touristenstraße · Pass	Tourist route · Pass
Schöner Ausblick · Rundblick · Landschaftlich bes. schöne Strecke	Scenic view · Panoramic view · Route with beautiful scenery
Heilbad · Schwimmbad	Spa · Swimming pool
Jugendherberge · Campingplatz	Youth hostel · Camping site
Golfplatz · Sprungschanze	Golf-course · Ski jump
Kirche im Ort, freistehend · Kapelle	Church · Chapel
Kloster · Klosterruine	Monastery · Monastery ruin
Synagoge · Moschee	Synagogue · Mosque
Schloss, Burg · Schloss-, Burgruine	Palace, castle · Ruin
Turm · Funk-, Fernsehturm	Tower · Radio-, TV-tower
Leuchtturm · Kraftwerk	Lighthouse · Power station
Wasserfall · Schleuse	Waterfall · Lock
Bauwerk · Marktplatz, Areal	Important building · Market place, area
Ausgrabungs- u. Ruinenstätte · Bergwerk	Arch. excavation, ruins · Mine
Dolmen · Menhir · Nuraghen	Dolmen · Menhir · Nuraghe
Hünen-, Hügelgrab · Soldatenfriedhof	Cairn · Military cemetery
Hotel, Gasthaus, Berghütte · Höhle	Hotel, inn, refuge · Cave

Kultur — **Culture**

Malerisches Ortsbild · Ortshöhe — **WIEN** (171) — Picturesque town · Elevation

Eine Reise wert — ★★ **MILANO** — Worth a journey

Lohnt einen Umweg — ★ **TEMPLIN** — Worth a detour

Sehenswert — Andermatt — Worth seeing

Landschaft — **Landscape**

Eine Reise wert — ★★ Las Cañadas — Worth a journey

Lohnt einen Umweg — ★ Texel — Worth a detour

Sehenswert — Dikti — Worth seeing

MARCO POLO Erlebnistour 1 — **MARCO POLO Discovery Tour 1**

MARCO POLO Erlebnistouren — **MARCO POLO Discovery Tours**

MARCO POLO Highlight — **MARCO POLO Highlight**

FOR YOUR NEXT TRIP...

MARCO POLO TRAVEL GUIDES

Algarve
Amsterdam
Andalucia
Athens
Australia
Austria
Bali & Lombok
Bangkok
Barcelona
Berlin
Brazil
Bruges
Brussels
Budapest
Bulgaria
California
Cambodia
Canada East
Canada West / Rockies & Vancouver
Cape Town & Garden Route
Cape Verde
Channel Islands
Chicago & The Lakes
China
Cologne
Copenhagen
Corfu
Costa Blanca & Valencia
Costa Brava
Costa del Sol & Granada
Costa Rica
Crete
Cuba
Cyprus (North and South)
Devon & Cornwall
Dresden
Dubai

Dublin
Dubrovnik & Dalmatian Coast
Edinburgh
Egypt
Egypt Red Sea Resorts
Finland
Florence
Florida
French Atlantic Coast
French Riviera (Nice, Cannes & Monaco)
Fuerteventura
Gran Canaria
Greece
Hamburg
Hong Kong & Macau
Ibiza
Iceland
India
India South
Ireland
Israel
Istanbul
Italy
Japan
Jordan
Kos
Krakow
Lake District
Lake Garda
Lanzarote
Las Vegas
Lisbon
London
Los Angeles
Madeira & Porto Santo
Madrid
Maldives
Mallorca
Malta & Gozo
Mauritius

Menorca
Milan
Montenegro
Morocco
Munich
Naples & Amalfi Coast
New York
New Zealand
Norway
Oslo
Oxford
Paris
Peru & Bolivia
Phuket
Portugal
Prague
Rhodes
Rome
Salzburg
San Francisco
Santorini
Sardinia
Scotland
Seychelles
Shanghai
Sicily
Singapore
South Africa
Sri Lanka
Stockholm
Switzerland
Tenerife
Thailand
Tokyo
Turkey
Turkey South Coast
Tuscany
United Arab Emirates
USA Southwest (Las Vegas, Colorado, New Mexico, Arizona & Utah)
Venice
Vienna
Vietnam
Zakynthos & Ithaca, Kefalonia, Lefkas

Travel with Insider Tips

INDEX

The index includes all the places, sights, museums, beaches and excursion destinations and beaches described in the guide. Page numbers in bold indicate the main entry.

Alderney Railway (A) 81, **82**
Alderney Society Museum (A) 83
Amaizin Adventure Park (J) 114
Ancresse Bay, L' (G) 69
Ancresse Common, L' (G) 70, 71
Anne Port (J) 46
Arcade (G) **73**, 77
Archirondel Tower (J) 52
Art Gallery (J) 75
Beaucette Marina (G) 71
Beauport (J) 49
Belcroute Bay (J) 48
Belvoir Bay (H) 91
Beresford Fish Market (J) 52
Bird Islands (A) 85
Bluebell Wood (G) **73**, 109
Bonne Nuit Bay (J) **41**, 43, 106
Bouley Bay (J) **41**, 43, 52, 106, 113
Braye Bay (A) 83, 86
Braye Harbour (A) 82, **83**, 85
Brecqhou (S) 92
Burhou (A) 85
Candie Gardens (G) **74**, 75, 76
Castel (G) 65, 67, 69, 116
Castle Cornet (G) **74**, 116
Central Market (J) 52
Cider Apple Orchard (J) 41
Cinema (A) 83
Clarence Battery (G) 108
Clonque Bay (A) 82
Cobo Bay (G) 65, 66, 67, **68**, 102, 115
Corbière Lighthouse (J) **34**, 100, 112
Corbière Point (J) 34
Corbière Railway Walk (J) 35, 99, 104
Corblets Bay (A) 84, 86, 113
Creux Harbour (S) 92
Déhus, Le (G) 16, **69**
Derrible Bay (S) 96
Devil's Hole (J) **39**, 101, 104
Dixcart Bay (S) 96
Dolmen de Faldouët (J) 44
Dolmen Le Déhus (G) 16, **69**
Dolmen Le Trépied (G) 65
Durrell Wildlife Conservation Trust (J) **39**, 43, 114, 116, 119
Elizabeth Castle (J) 51, **52**
Eperquerie Landing (S) 96
Eric Young Orchid Foundation (J) 57
Etacs, Les (A) 85
Faldouët (J) 44
Fermain Bay (G) **64**, 109
Fishermen's Chapel (J) 48
Fliquet Bay (J) 57
Folk and Costume Museum (G) 66

Forest (G) 60, 61, 65
Fort Clonque (A) 84
Fort Corblets (A) 84
Fort Doyle (A) 84
Fort Field (G) 71
Fort George (G) 109
Fort Grey (G) **65**, 102
Fort Leicester (J) 52
Fort Pembroke (G) 71
Fort Regent (J) 51
Fort Saumarez (G) 66
Fort Tourgis (A) 84
Fouaillages, Les (G) 70
German Military Underground Hospital (G) 61
German Occupation Museum (G) **61**, 66
Gorey (J) 43, 44, 45, 46, 101
Gouliot Caves (S) 92
Gouliot Passage (S) 92
Grand Havre (G) **71**, 72, 102
Grande Grève, La (S) 96
Grande Route des Mielles, La (J) **35**, 36, 101, 113
Grandmère du Chimquière, La (G) 61
Green Island (J) 55
Grève de Lecq (J) **41**, 42, 101, 104, 113
Grosnez Castle (J) 35
Grosnez Point (J) 35
Guernsey Museum & Art Gallery (G) **75**, 76
Guernsey Tapestry, The (G) 75
Hamptonne Country Life Museum (J) **47**, 52, 103
Hauteville House (G) **75**, 102
Havre de Fer (J) 46
Havre des Pas (J) 56, 101, **114**
Herm Harbour (H) 90
Hougue Bie, La (J) 57
Icart Point (G) **63**, 64, 65
Icho Tower (J) 55
Jerbourg Point (G) 62
Jersey Lavender (J) 27, **47**
Jersey Museum & Art Gallery (J) 24, **53**
Jersey Turbot Farm (J) 44
Jersey War Tunnels (J) 47
Jersey's Living Legend Village (J) 47
Judith Quérée (J) 35
King Street (J) 55
L'Étacq (J) 36, 57, 101, 112
L'Etacquerel Fort (J) 52, 107
La Coupe Point (J) 57
La Coupée (S) 92, **93**, 96, 103
La Crête Fort (J) **43**, 106
La Mare Wine Estate (J) 29, 31, **40**, 104

La Varde (G) 70
Ladies' Bay (G) 70, **71**
Le Déhus (G) 16, **69**
Le Noir Pré (J) 23, **36**, 116
Liberty Wharf (J) 30, **55**, 56
Lihou Island (G) 66
Little Chapel (G) 61
Little Sark (S) **92**, 95, 96, 97, 103
Longis Bay (A) **83**, 86
Longis Nature Reserve (A) 83
Manoir, Le (H) 90
Manor House (H) 90
Maritime Museum (G) 75
Maritime Museum (J) 53
Maseline Harbour (S) 92, **93**
Mielles, Les (J) 34, 36
Mont Orgueil Castle (J) **44**, 101
Moulin de Quetivel, Le (J) 48
Moulin Huet Bay (G) 60, 62, **63**, 64
Museum of the Royal Guernsey Militia (G) 75
Noir Pré, Le (J) 23, **36**, 116
Noirmont Point (J) **48**, 49, 57, 112
Nunnery (A) 84
Oatlands Village (G) 115
Occupation Tapestry Gallery (J) 53
Ortac (A) 85
Ouaisné Bay (J) 47, 48, **49**, 57
Ozanne Steps (G) 109
Pembroke Bay (G) **71**, 72
Perelle Bay (G) 65
Petit Bôt Bay (G) 63
Pinacle, Le (J) 35
Pleinmont Plateau (G) 66
Pleinmont Tower (G) 66
Plémont Bay (J) **42**, 101, 113
Point Robert (S) 93
Point Sauzebourge (H) 90
Port du Moulin (S) 94
Port Gorey (S) 96
Port Grat (J) 71
Port Soif (G) 71, **72**
Portelet Bay (G) 64
Portelet Bay (J) **48**, **49**, 57
Portelet Common (J) 48, 50, 57
Portelet Harbour (G) 65, 69
Portinfer Bay (G) 72
Prison (S) 94
Rocco Tower, La (J) **36**, 52
Rosaire Steps (H) 90
Rousse Tower (G) **71**, 102
Royal Bay of Grouville (J) 43, **45**, 52, 55, 57, 112
Royal Court (G) 75
Rozel Bay (J) 27, 40, **42**, 43, 107

Saints Bay (G) **63**, **64**, 65
Saline Bay (A) 86
Saline Bay (G) 68
Samarès Manor (J) 57
Sark Occupation & Heritage Museum (S) 94
Saumarez Park (G) 66
Sausmarez Manor (G) **62**, 102, 115
Saye Bay (A) 85, 86
Seigneurie, La (S) **94**, 102
Seymour Tower (J) 52, 55
Shell Beach (H) 31, **91**
Shipwreck Museum (G) **65**, 102
Sorel Point (J) **39**, 112
St Andrew (G) 60
St Anne (A) 83, **84**, 85, 86, 87
St Apolline's Chapel (G) 67
St Aubin (J) 27, 46, 47, 48, 49, 50, 51, 99, 103
St Aubin's Bay (J) 47, 48, 49, **50**, 117
St Aubin's Fort (J) **48**, 99
St Brelade (J) 51
St Brelade's Bay (J) 18, 47, **50**, 51, 57, 113, 115
St Brelade's Parish Church (J) 48
St Catherine's Bay (J) 46
St Catherine's Breakwater (J) **44**, 57, 112
St Helier (J) 19, 26, 28, 30, 31, 46, 47, **51**, 52, 101, 112, 113, 114, 117, 122
St John (J) 39, 104, 113
St Lawrence (J) 47, 114
St Martin (G) 60, 62, 63, 64, 65, 113
St Martin (J) 46
St Mary (J) 39
St Ouen (J) 34
St Ouen's Bay (J) 23, 27, 33, **37**, 38, 52, 100, 104, 112, 113
St Ouen's Pond (J) 34, 38
St Peter (J) 34, 37, 47, 114
St Peter Port (G) 16, 30, 31, 63, 64, **72**, 102, 108, 112, 113, 116, 122
St Peter-in-the-Wood (G) 65
St Peter's Church (S) 94
St Peter's Valley (J) 47, 48
St Sampson (G) 64, 69, 72, 115
St Saviour (G) 63, 65
St Saviour (J) 19, 54
St Tugual's Chapel (H) 90
St-Pierre-du-Bois (G) 65
Tamba Park (J) 114
Telegraph Bay (A) 85
Torteval (G) 60
Town Church (G) 75
Trépied, Le (G) 65
Trinity (J) 39

134

CREDITS

Val du Saou (A) 85
Vale (G) 19, 69, 71, 72
Vale Castle (G) 70
Valette Bathing Pools, La (G) 108
Valette Underground Military Museum, La (G) 31, **76**, 108
Variouf, Le (G) 63

Vazon Bay (G) **68**, 113
Venus Pool (G) 93, 96, 103
Victor Hugo's House (G) **75**, 102
Victoria Tower (G) 76
Victoria Tower (J) 44
Victorian forts (A) 24, 82, **84**
Victorian Shop (G) 76

Waterworks Valley (J) 47, 103
Wetland Centre (J) 36
White Rock (J) 112
Wildlife Trust Bunker (A) 85
Windmill (S) 94
Window in the Rock (S) 94, 102

WRITE TO US

e-mail: sales@heartwoodpublishing.co.uk

Did you have a great holiday? Is there something on your mind? Whatever it is, let us know! Whether you want to praise, alert us to errors or give us a personal tip – MARCO POLO would be pleased to hear from you.

We do everything we can to provide the very latest information for your trip. Nevertheless, despite all of our authors' thorough research, errors can creep in. MARCO POLO does not accept any ability for this. Please contact us by e-mail.

PICTURE CREDITS
Cover photograph: Portelet Bay on Jersey (Schapowalow/SIME: G. Simeone)
Photos: Corbis/JAI: N. Farrin (29); DuMont Bildarchiv: R. Kiedrowski (22, 62, 82, 113, 115, 118 top); f1online (68/69); Getty Images: D. Clapp (49), A. Lagadu (117), M. Robertson (flap right); Getty Images/Images Etc Ltd (7); Getty Images/PM Images (116/117); Getty Images/Westend61 (3); U. Haafke (114/115); huber-images: R. Birkby (128/129), D. A´Anna (104), O. Fantuz (4 bottom, 12/13, 32/33, 58/59), J. Foulkes (34), G. Santoni (74), R. Schmid (20/21, 26/27), R. Taylor (2, 50, 98/99, 107); Jersey Tourism (116); S. Kuttig (114); Laif: M. Amme (4 top, 56, 78, 110/111), E. Bock (88/89, 95), Ch. Boisvieux (93), F. Heuer (112), F. Jaenicke (5, 90), Ch. Kaiser (14/15, 118 bottom); Laif/hemis.fr: R. Manin (53), B. Rieger (46), J.-D. Sudres (18 centre, 97); Laif/Robert Harding: M. Runkel (80/81); Look/age fotostock (17); Marine Conservation Society: Jacki Clark (18 bottom); mauritius images: E. Gebhardt (18 top); mauritius images/age (72/73, 108/109); mauritius images/Alamy (28 left, 28 right), D. Askham (19 top), G. Brown (65), D. Houghton (11, 67), J. Kruse (6, 45), B. Moore (9), G. Shoosmith (37), J. Tack (25, 70), T. Whitefoot (86/87); mauritius images/Alamy/Eyebyte (39); mauritius images/Alamy/nobleIMAGES (60); mauritius images/go-images (19 bottom); mauritius images/imagebroker: D. Renckhoff (30/31); A. Mockford & N. Bonetti (54, 76); D. Renckhoff (8, 10, 30, 31, 42); Schapowalow/4Corners: R. Birkby (flap left, 119); Schapowalow/SIME: G. Simeone (1 top); O. Stadler (84); vario images/FLPA (40)

2nd edition – fully revised and updated 2020
Worldwide Distribution: Marco Polo Travel Publishing Ltd, Pinewood, Chineham Business Park, Crockford Lane, Basingstoke, Hampshire RG24 8AL, United Kingdom. Email: sales@marcopolouk.com
© MAIRDUMONT GmbH & Co. KG , Ostfildern
Chief editor: Stefanie Penck
Author: Martin Müller; editor: Nikolai Michaelis; picture editor: Veronika Plajer; What's hot: Martin Müller/wunder media, Munich
Cartography road atlas and pull-out map: © MAIRDUMONT, Ostfildern
Cover design, p. 1, pull-out map cover: Karl Anders – Studio für Brand Profiling, Hamburg
Design inside: milchhof:atelier, Berlin; design p. 2/3, Discovery Tours: Susan Chaaban Dipl.-Des. (FH)
Translated from German by Jonathan Andrews and Dr. Suzanne Kirkbright
Editorial office: SAW Communications, Redaktionsbüro Dr. Sabine A. Werner, Mainz: Frauke Feuchter, Julia Gilcher, Dr. Sabine A. Werner; prepress: SAW Communications, Mainz,
in cooperation with alles mit Medien, Mainz
All rights reserved. No part of this book may be reproduced, stored in a retrieval system or transmitted in any form or by any means (electronic, mechanical, photocopying, recording or otherwise) without prior written permission from the publisher.
Printed in India

MIX
Paper from responsible sources
FSC® C016779

DOS & DON'TS

A couple of tips so you don't ruin your clothes or the atmosphere

SWIM WITHOUT THINKING

The tides and currents in the English Channel are swift and overpowering. That means you should only swim on supervised beaches that are marked as being safe. You can find out when it's safe to walk along the coasts by taking a look at the tide tables – you'll find them at Tourist Information centres and in many hotels and pubs on the islands.

TRAVEL BY CAR ON THE ISLANDS

The roads on the Channel Islands are narrow and winding. If you're planning to make a detour to the islands from France, it's probably better if you don't bring your car. If you want to get around on Jersey and Guernsey, it's best to rent bikes or make use of the buses that travel all over the islands. If you really want to bring a car with you, be sure to take care on junctions marked "Filter In Turn". No car has priority in this zipper-like system, and you should try to tuck in quickly when cars let you pass.

GET TOO CLOSE TO THE BIRDS

Numerous bird species nest on the Channel Islands from May to July. In some places, you'll feel like you're in a scene from Alfred Hitchcock's famous thriller. Seagulls, guillemots, auks, shags and many more besides raise their families on the cliffs, and masses of puffins chatter on a rock off the coast of Alderney. But beware: disgruntled great black-backed gulls defend their breeding grounds by nose diving birdwatchers. At least you'll see them coming: by the time you know you've annoyed a fulmar, it'll already be too late. These taciturn, aerobatic birds like to nest just where hikers place their feet. And they won't let you get away with trampling near their homes: they attack by spitting a regurgitated stink bomb over 2 m/6.6 ft. The resulting oily stains ruin trousers and stink to high heaven. The areas around their nests on the slopes and beaches are covered in splashes from previous attacks.

WORRY ABOUT DISCUSSING SECOND WORLD WAR

Although the Channel Islands were deeply affected, you shouldn't worry about discussing the war. The five years of German occupation didn't just leave traces of concrete behind – the war museums display a real passion for the era's history. Most locals look back at the time without resentment.

MISS SARK'S COMMUNITY NEWSLETTER

The Sark Newspaper, written by the Barclay Brothers' representatives, shouldn't be taken seriously as a work of journalism. It does make for interesting reading, however, and gives an insight into what really gets the blood boiling in this formerly undisturbed feudal island community. Every edition is a new episode in the dramatic soap opera of life on Sark.